The Missionary by William Lisle Bowles

William Lisle Bowles was born on 24th September 1762 at King's Sutton in Northamptonshire.

His great-grandfather, grandfather and his father, William Thomas Bowles, had all been parish priests and inevitably Bowles would join their line.

In 1789 Bowles published, a small quarto volume, Fourteen Sonnets, which was received with extraordinary praise, not only by the general public, but by such revered poets as Samuel Taylor Coleridge and Wordsworth.

After receiving his degree at Oxford, Bowles now began his career in service to the Church of England.

His years of service perhaps diminished both his stature as a poet and certainly the way he was viewed. For much of his career Bowles was seen as rather soft when set against his contemporaries but in the end his ability as a poet was enshrined, after a long and ferocious attack against him, by the principles he so eloquently wrote about and adhered too.

In personality and nature Bowles was said to be an amiable, absent-minded, but rather eccentric man. His poems speak warmly of a refinement of feeling, tenderness, and pensive thought, but are lacking in power and passion. But that should not diminish their value or appreciation to us.

Bowles maintained that images drawn from nature are poetically finer than those drawn from art; and that in the highest kinds of poetry the themes or passions handled should be of the general or elemental kind, and not the transient manners of any society.

As well as his poetry Bowles was also responsible for writing a Life of Bishop Ken (in two volumes, 1830–1831), Coombe Ellen and St. Michael's Mount (1798), The Battle of the Nile (1799), and The Sorrows of Switzerland (1801).

William Lisle Bowles died on April 7th, 1850 at the age of 87.

Index of Contents
Preface to the Second Edition
Scene
Characters
Introduction
CANTO FIRST
Argument
CANTO SECOND
Argument
CANTO THIRD
Argument
CANTO FOURTH
Argument

CANTO FIFTH
Argument
CANTO SIXTH
Argument
CANTO SEVENTH
Argument
CANTO EIGHTH
Argument
William Lisle Bowles - A Short Biography

Amor patriæ ratione potentior omni.

PREFACE TO THE SECOND EDITION

It is not necessary to relate the causes which induced me to publish this poem without a name.

The favour with which it has been received may make me less diffident in avowing it; and, as a second edition has been generally called for, I have endeavoured to make it, in every respect, less unworthy of the public eye.

I have availed myself of every sensible objection, the most material of which was the circumstance, that the Indian maid, described in the first book, had not a part assigned to her of sufficient interest in the subsequent events of the poem, and that the character of the Missionary was not sufficiently professional.

The single circumstance that a Spanish commander, with his army in South America, was destroyed by the Indians, in consequence of the treachery of his page, who was a native, and that only a priest was saved, is all that has been taken from history. The rest of this poem, the personages, father, daughter, wife, et cet. (with the exception of the names of Indian warriors) is imaginary. The time is two months. The first four books include as many days and nights. The rest of the time is occupied by the Spaniards' march, the assembly of warriors, et cet.

The place in which the scene is laid, was selected because South America has of late years received additional interest, and because the ground was at once new, poetical, and picturesque.

From old-fashioned feelings, perhaps, I have admitted some aërial agents, or what is called machinery. It is true that the spirits cannot be said to accelerate or retard the events; but surely they may be allowed to show a sympathy with the fate of those, among whom poetical fancy has given them a prescriptive ideal existence. They may be further excused, as relieving the narrative, and adding to the imagery.

The causes which induced me to publish this poem without a name, induced me also to attempt it in a versification to which I have been least accustomed, which, to my ear, is most uncongenial, and which is, in itself, most difficult. I mention this, in order that, if some passages should be found less harmonious than they might have been, the candour of the reader may pardon them.

THE MISSIONARY

SCENE—SOUTH AMERICA.

CHARACTERS
Valdivia, commander of the Spanish armies
Lautaro, his page, a native of Chili
Anselmo, the missionary
Indiana, his adopted daughter, wife of Lautaro
Zarinel, the wandering minstrel.

Indians.
Attacapac, father of Lautaro
Olola, his daughter, sister of Lautaro
Caupolican, chief of the Indians—
Indian warriors.

The chief event of the poem turns upon the conduct of Lautaro; but as the Missionary acts so distinguished a part, and as the whole of the moral depends upon him, it was thought better to retain the title which was originally given to the poem.

Dedicated to the Marquis of Lansdowne

INTRODUCTION

When o'er the Atlantic wild, rocked by the blast,
Sad Lusitania's exiled sovereign passed,
Reft of her pomp, from her paternal throne
Cast forth, and wandering to a clime unknown,
To seek a refuge on that distant shore,
That once her country's legions dyed with gore;—
Sudden, methought, high towering o'er the flood,
Hesperian world! thy mighty genius stood;
Where spread, from cape to cape, from bay to bay,
Serenely blue, the vast Pacific lay;
And the huge Cordilleras to the skies
With all their burning summits seemed to rise.
Then the stern spirit spoke, and to his voice
The waves and woods replied:—Mountains, rejoice!
Thou solitary sea, whose billows sweep
The margin of my forests, dark and deep,
Rejoice! the hour is come: the mortal blow,
That smote the golden shrines of Mexico,
In Europe is avenged; and thou, proud Spain,
Now hostile hosts insult thy own domain;

Now Fate, vindictive, rolls, with refluent flood,
Back on thy shores the tide of human blood,
Think of my murdered millions! of the cries
That once I heard from all my kingdoms rise;
Of Famine's feeble plaint, of Slavery's tear;—
Think, too, if Valour, Freedom, Fame, be dear,
How my Antarctic sons, undaunted, stood,
Exacting groan for groan, and blood for blood;
And shouted, (may the sounds be hailed by thee!)
Tyrants, the virtuous and the brave are free!

CANTO FIRST

ARGUMENT

One Day and Part of Night

Valley in the Andes—Old Indian warrior—Loss of his son and daughter

Beneath aërial cliffs, and glittering snows,
The rush-roof of an aged warrior rose,
Chief of the mountain tribes: high overhead,
The Andes, wild and desolate, were spread,
Where cold Sierras shot their icy spires,
And Chillan trailed its smoke and smouldering fires.
A glen beneath, a lonely spot of rest,
Hung, scarce discovered, like an eagle's nest.

Summer was in its prime;—the parrot-flocks
Darkened the passing sunshine on the rocks;
The chrysomel and purple butterfly,
Amid the clear blue light, are wandering by;
The humming-bird, along the myrtle bowers,
With twinkling wing, is spinning o'er the flowers,
The woodpecker is heard with busy bill,
The mock-bird sings—and all beside is still,
And look! the cataract that bursts so high,
As not to mar the deep tranquillity,
The tumult of its dashing fall suspends,
And, stealing drop by drop, in mist descends;
Through whose illumined spray and sprinkling dews,
Shine to the adverse sun the broken rainbow hues.

Chequering, with partial shade, the beams of noon,
And arching the gray rock with wild festoon,
Here its gay net-work, and fantastic twine,
The purple cogul threads from pine to pine,

And oft, as the fresh airs of morning breathe,
Dips its long tendrils in the stream beneath.
There, through the trunks with moss and lichens white,
The sunshine darts its interrupted light,
And, 'mid the cedar's darksome boughs, illumes,
With instant touch, the Lori's scarlet plumes.

So smiles the scene;—but can its smiles impart
Aught to console yon mourning warrior's heart?
He heeds not now, when beautifully bright,
The humming-bird is circling in his sight;
Nor ev'n, above his head, when air is still,
Hears the green woodpecker's resounding bill;
But gazing on the rocks and mountains wild,
Rock after rock, in glittering masses piled
To the volcano's cone, that shoots so high
Gray smoke whose column stains the cloudless sky,
He cries, Oh! if thy spirit yet be fled
To the pale kingdoms of the shadowy dead,—
In yonder tract of purest light above,
Dear long-lost object of a father's love,
Dost thou abide; or like a shadow come,
Circling the scenes of thy remembered home,
And passing with the breeze, or, in the beam
Of evening, light the desert mountain stream!
Or at deep midnight are thine accents heard,
In the sad notes of that melodious bird,
Which, as we listen with mysterious dread,
Brings tidings from our friends and fathers dead?
Perhaps, beyond those summits, far away,
Thine eyes yet view the living light of day;
Sad, in the stranger's land, thou may'st sustain
A weary life of servitude and pain,
With wasted eye gaze on the orient beam,
And think of these white rocks and torrent stream,
Never to hear the summer cocoa wave,
Or weep upon thy father's distant grave.

Ye, who have waked, and listened with a tear,
When cries confused, and clangours rolled more near;
With murmured prayer, when Mercy stood aghast,
As War's black trump pealed its terrific blast,
And o'er the withered earth the armed giant passed!
Ye, who his track with terror have pursued,
When some delightful land, all blood-imbrued,
He swept; where silent is the champaign wide,
That echoed to the pipe of yester-tide,
Save, when far off, the moonlight hills prolong

The last deep echoes of his parting gong;
Nor aught is seen, in the deserted spot
Where trailed the smoke of many a peaceful cot,
Save livid corses that unburied lie,
And conflagrations, reeking to the sky;—
Come listen, whilst the causes I relate
That bowed the warrior to the storms of fate,
And left these smiling scenes forlorn and desolate.

In other days, when, in his manly pride,
Two children for a father's fondness vied,—
Oft they essayed, in mimic strife, to wield
His lance, or laughing peeped behind his shield;
Oft in the sun, or the magnolia's shade,
Lightsome of heart as gay of look they played,
Brother and sister. She, along the dew,
Blithe as the squirrel of the forest flew;
Blue rushes wreathed her head; her dark-brown hair
Fell, gently lifted, on her bosom bare;
Her necklace shone, of sparkling insects made,
That flit, like specks of fire, from sun to shade.
Light was her form; a clasp of silver braced
The azure-dyed ichella round her waist;
Her ancles rung with shells, as unconfined
She danced, and sung wild carols to the wind.
With snow-white teeth, and laughter in her eye,
So beautiful in youth she bounded by.

Yet kindness sat upon her aspect bland,—
The tame alpaca stood and licked her hand;
She brought him gathered moss, and loved to deck
With flowery twine his tall and stately neck,
Whilst he with silent gratitude replies,
And bends to her caress his large blue eyes.

These children danced together in the shade,
Or stretched their hands to see the rainbow fade;
Or sat and mocked, with imitative glee,
The paroquet, that laughed from tree to tree;
Or through the forest's wildest solitude,
From glen to glen, the marmozet pursued;
And thought the light of parting day too short,
That called them, lingering, from their daily sport.

In that fair season of awakening life,
When dawning youth and childhood are at strife;
When on the verge of thought gay boyhood stands
Tiptoe, with glistening eye and outspread hands;

With airy look, and form and footsteps light,
And glossy locks, and features berry-bright,
And eye like the young eaglet's, to the ray
Of noon unblenching as he sails away;
A brede of sea-shells on his bosom strung,
A small stone-hatchet o'er his shoulder slung,
With slender lance, and feathers blue and red,
That, like the heron's crest, waved on his head,—
Buoyant with hope, and airiness, and joy,
Lautaro was a graceful Indian boy:
Taught by his sire, ev'n now he drew the bow,
Or tracked the jagguar on the morning snow;
Startled the condor, on the craggy height;
Then silent sat, and marked its upward flight,
Lessening in ether to a speck of white.

But when the impassioned chieftain spoke of war,
Smote his broad breast, or pointed to a scar,—
Spoke of the strangers of the distant main,
And the proud banners of insulting Spain,—
Of the barbed horse and iron horseman spoke,
And his red gods, that, wrapped in rolling smoke,
Roared from the guns;—the boy, with still-drawn breath,
Hung on the wondrous tale, as mute as death;
Then raised his animated eyes, and cried,
Oh, let me perish by my father's side!

Once, when the moon, o'er Chillan's cloudless height,
Poured, far and wide, its softest, mildest light,
A predatory band of mailed men
Burst on the stillness of the sheltered glen:
They shouted, Death! and shook their sabres high,
That shone terrific to the moonlight sky;
Where'er they rode, the valley and the hill
Echoed the shrieks of death, till all again was still.

The warrior, ere he sank in slumber deep,
Had kissed his son, soft-breathing in his sleep,
Where on a Llama's skin he lay, and said,
Placing his hand, with tears, upon his head,
Aërial nymphs! that in the moonlight stray,
O gentle spirits! here awhile delay;
Bless, as ye pass unseen, my sleeping boy,
Till blithe he wakes to daylight and to joy.
If the GREAT SPIRIT will, in future days,
O'er the fall'n foe his hatchet he shall raise,
And, 'mid a grateful nation's high applause,
Avenge his violated country's cause!

Now, nearer points of spears, and many a cone
Of moving helmets, in the moonlight shone,
As, clanking through the pass, the band of blood
Sprang, like hyænas, from the secret wood.
They rush, they seize their unresisting prey,
Ruthless they tear the shrieking boy away;
But, not till gashed by many a sabre wound,
The father sank, expiring, on the ground.
He waked from the dark trance to life and pain,
But never saw his darling child again.

Seven snows had fallen, and seven green summers passed,
Since here he heard that son's loved accents last.
Still his beloved daughter soothed his cares,
Whilst time began to strew with white his hairs.
Oft as his painted feathers he unbound,
Or gazed upon his hatchet on the ground,
Musing with deep despair, nor strove to speak,
Light she approached, and climbed to reach his cheek,
Held with both hands his forehead, then her head
Drew smiling back, and kissed the tear he shed.

But late, to grief and hopeless love a prey,
She left his side, and wandered far away.
Now in this still and shelter'd glen, that smiled
Beneath the crags of precipices wild,
Wrapt in a stern yet sorrowful repose,
The warrior half forgot his country's woes;
Forgot how many, impotent to save,
Shed their best blood upon a father's grave;
How many, torn from wife and children, pine
In the dark caverns of the hopeless mine,
Never to see again the blessed morn;—
Slaves in the lovely land where they were born;
How many at sad sunset, with a tear,
The distant roar of sullen cannons hear,
Whilst evening seems, as dies the sound, to throw
A deadlier stillness on a nation's woe!

So the dark warrior, day succeeding day,
Wore in distempered thought the noons away;
And still, when weary evening came, he sighed,
My son, my son! or, with emotion, cried,
When I descend to the cold grave alone,
Who shall be there to mourn for me?—Not one!
The crimson orb of day now westering flung
His beams, and o'er the vast Pacific hung;

When from afar a shrilling sound was heard,
And, hurrying o'er the dews, a scout appeared.
The watchful warrior knew the piercing tones,
The signal-call of war, from human bones,—
What tidings? with impatient look, he cried.
Tidings of war, the hurrying scout replied;
Then the sharp pipe with shriller summons blew,
And held the blood-red arrow high in view.

CHIEF
Where speed the foes?

INDIAN
Along the southern main,
Have passed the vultures of accursed Spain.

CHIEF
Ruin pursue them on the distant flood,
And be their deadly portion—blood for blood!

INDIAN
When, round and red, the moon shall next arise,
The chiefs attend the midnight sacrifice
In Encol's wood, where the great wizard dwells,
Who wakes the dead man by his thrilling spells;
Thee, Ulmen of the Mountains, they command
To lift the hatchet for thy native land;
Whilst in dread circle, round the sere-wood smoke,
The mighty gods of vengeance they invoke;
And call the spirits of their fathers slain,
To nerve their lifted arm, and curse devoted Spain.

So spoke the scout of war;—and o'er the dew,
Onward along the craggy valley, flew.
Then the stern warrior sang his song of death—
And blew his conch, that all the glens beneath
Echoed, and rushing from the hollow wood,
Soon at his side three hundred warriors stood.

WARRIOR
Children, who for his country dares to die?

Three hundred brandished spears shone to the sky:
We perish, or we leave our country free;
Father, our blood for Chili and for thee!
The mountain-chief essayed his club to wield,
And shook the dust indignant from the shield.
Then spoke:—

O Thou! that with thy lingering light
Dost warm the world, till all is hushed in night;
I look upon thy parting beams, O sun!
And say, ev'n thus my course is almost run.
When thou dost hide thy head, as in the grave,
And sink to glorious rest beneath the wave,
Dost thou, majestic in repose, retire,
Below the deep, to unknown worlds of fire!
Yet though thou sinkest, awful, in the main,
The shadowy moon comes forth, and all the train
Of stars, that shine with soft and silent light,
Making so beautiful the brow of night.
Thus, when I sleep within the narrow bed,
The light of after-fame around shall spread;
The sons of distant Ocean, when they see
The grass-green heap beneath the mountain tree,
And hear the leafy boughs at evening wave,
Shall pause and say, There sleep in dust the brave!

All earthly hopes my lonely heart have fled!
Stern Guecubu, angel of the dead,
Who laughest when the brave in pangs expire;
Whose dwelling is beneath the central fire
Of yonder burning mountain; who hast passed
O'er my poor dwelling, and with one fell blast
Scattered my summer-leaves that clustered round,
And swept my fairest blossoms to the ground;
Angel of dire despair, oh! come not nigh,
Nor wave thy red wings o'er me where I lie;
But thou, O mild and gentle spirit! stand,
Angel of hope and peace, at my right hand,
(When blood-drops stagnate on my brow) and guide
My pathless voyage o'er the unknown tide,
To scenes of endless joy, to that fair isle,
Where bowers of bliss, and soft savannahs smile:
Where my forefathers oft the fight renew,
And Spain's black visionary steeds pursue;
Where, ceased the struggles of all human pain,
I may behold thee—thee, my son, again!

He spoke, and whilst at evening's glimmering close
The distant mist, like the gray ocean, rose,
With patriot sorrows swelling at his breast,
He sank upon a jagguar's hide to rest.

'Twas night: remote on Caracalla's bay,
Valdivia's army, hushed in slumber, lay.

Around the limits of the silent camp,
Alone was heard the steed's patroling tramp
From line to line, whilst the fixed sentinel
Proclaimed the watch of midnight—All is well!
Valdivia dreamed of millions yet untold,
Villrica's gems, and El Dorado's gold!

What different feelings, by the scene impressed,
Rose in sad tumult o'er Lautaro's breast!
On the broad ocean, where the moonlight slept,
Thoughtful he turned his waking eyes, and wept,
And whilst the thronging forms of memory start,
Thus holds communion with his lonely heart:

Land of my fathers, still I tread your shore,
And mourn the shade of hours that are no more;
Whilst night-airs, like remembered voices, sweep,
And murmur from the undulating deep.
Was it thy voice, my father! Thou art dead,
The green rush waves on thy forsaken bed.
Was it thy voice, my sister! Gentle maid,
Thou too, perhaps, in the dark cave art laid;
Perhaps, even now, thy spirit sees me stand
A homeless stranger in my native land;
Perhaps, even now, along the moonlight sea,
It bends from the blue cloud, remembering me!
Land of my fathers! yet, oh yet forgive,
That with thy deadly enemies I live:
The tenderest ties (it boots not to relate)
Have bound me to their service, and their fate;
Yet, whether on Peru's war-wasted plain,
Or visiting these sacred shores again,
Whate'er the struggles of this heart may be,
Land of my fathers, it shall beat for thee!

NOTES

A volcano in Chili.

The chrysomela is a beautiful insect of which the young women of Chili make necklaces.

The parrot butterfly, peculiar to this part of America, the largest and most brilliant of its kind.—Papilio psittacus.

A most beautiful climbing plant. The vine is of the size of packthread: it climbs on the trees without attaching itself to them: when it reaches the top, it descends perpendicularly; and as it continues to grow, it extends itself from tree to tree, until it offers to the eye a confused tissue, exhibiting some resemblance to the rigging of a ship.—Molina.

I chanced once to lodge in a village named Upec by the Frenchmen: there, in the night, I heard those birds, not singing, but making a lamentable noise. I saw the barbarians most attentive, and, being ignorant of the whole matter, reproved their folly. But when I smiled a little upon a Frenchman standing by me, a certain old man, severely enough, restrained me with these words: "Hold your peace, lest you hinder us who attentively hearken to the happy tidings of our ancestors; for as often as we hear these birds, so often also are we cheered, and our strength receiveth increase."—Callender's Voyage.

The ichella is a short cloak, of a greenish-blue colour, of wool, fastened before with a silver buckle.—Molina.

The alpaca is perhaps the most beautiful, gentle, and interesting of living animals: one was to be seen in London in .

Ardea cristata.

Every warrior of Chili, according to Molina, has his attendant "nymph" or fairy—the belief in which is nearly similar to the popular and poetical idea of those beings in Europe. Meulen is the benevolent spirit.

I have taken this line from the conclusion of the celebrated speech of the old North American warrior, Logan, "Who is there to mourn for Logan?—not one!"

Their pipes of war are made of the bones of their enemies, who have been sacrificed.

The way in which the warriors are summoned, is something like the "running the cross" in Scotland, which is so beautifully described by Walter Scott. The scouts on this occasion bear an arrow bound with red fillets.

Ulmen is the same as Casique, or chief.

Guecubu{h} is the evil spirit of the Chilians.

They have their evil and good spirits.

CANTO SECOND

ARGUMENT

The Second Day

Night—Spirit of the Andes—Valdivia—Lautaro—Missionary—The   Hermitage

The night was still and clear, when, o'er the snows,
Andes! thy melancholy Spirit rose,—

A shadow stern and sad: he stood alone,
Upon the topmost mountain's burning cone;
And whilst his eyes shone dim, through surging smoke,
Thus to the spirits of the fire he spoke:—

Ye, who tread the hidden deeps,
Where the silent earthquake sleeps;
Ye, who track the sulphurous tide,
Or on hissing vapours ride,—
Spirits, come!
From worlds of subterraneous night;
From fiery realms of lurid light;
From the ore's unfathomed bed;
From the lava's whirlpools red,—
Spirits, come!
On Chili's foes rush with vindictive sway,
And sweep them from the light of living day!
Heard ye not the ravenous brood,
That flap their wings, and scream for blood?
On Peru's devoted shore
Their murderous beaks are red with gore;
Yet here, impatient for new prey,
The insatiate vultures track their way.
Let them perish! they, whose bands
Swept remote and peaceful lands!
Let them perish!—on their head,
Descend the darkness of the dead!
Spirits, now your caves forsake:
Hark! ten thousand warriors wake!—
Spirits, their high cause defend!—
From your caves ascend! ascend!

As thus the Genius of the Andes spoke,
The trembling mountain heaved with darker smoke;
Lightnings, and phantom-forms, by fits appeared;
His mighty voice far off Osorno heard;
The caverned deeps shook through their vast profound,
And Chimborazzo's height rolled back the sound.

With lifted arm, and towering stature high,
And aspect frowning to the middle sky
(Its misty form dilated in the wind),
The phantom stood,—till, less and less defined,
Into thin air it faded from the sight,
Lost in the ambient haze of slow-returning light.
Its feathery-seeming crown, its giant spear,
Its limbs of huge proportion, disappear;
And the bare mountains to the dawn disclose

The same long line of solitary snows.

The morning shines, the military train
Streams far and wide along the tented plain;
And plaited cuirasses, and helms of steel,
Throw back the sunbeams, as the horsemen wheel:
Thus, with arms glancing to the eastern light,
Pass, in review, proud steeds and cohorts bright;
For all the host, by break of morrow's gray,
Wind back their march to Penco's northern bay,
Valdivia, fearful lest confederate foes,
Ambushed and dark, his progress might oppose,
Marshals to-day the whole collected force,
File and artillery, cuirassier and horse:
Himself yet lingers ere he joins the train,
That moves, in ordered march, along the plain,
While troops, and Indian slaves beneath his eye,
The labours of the rising city ply:
Wide glows the general toil; the mole extends,
The watch-tower o'er the desert surge ascends;
And battlements, and rising ramparts, shine
Above the ocean's blue and level line.

The sun ascended to meridian height,
And all the northern bastions shone in light;
With hoarse acclaim, the gong and trumpet rung,
The Moorish slaves aloft their cymbals swung,
When the proud victor, in triumphant state,
Rode forth, in arms, through the portcullis' gate.

With neck high-arching as he smote the ground,
And restless pawing to the trumpet's sound,—
With mantling mane, o'er his broad shoulders spread,
And nostrils blowing, and dilated red,—
The coal-black steed, in rich caparison
Far trailing to the ground, went proudly on.
Proudly he tramped, as conscious of his charge,
And turned around his eye-balls, bright and large,
And shook the frothy boss, as in disdain;
And tossed the flakes, indignant, off his mane;
And, with high-swelling veins, exulting pressed
Proudly against the barb his heaving breast.

The fate of empires glowing in his thought,
Thus armed, the tented field Valdivia sought.
On the left side his poised shield he bore,
With quaint devices richly blazoned o'er;
Above the plumes, upon his helmet's cone,

Castile's imperial crest illustrious shone;
Blue in the wind the escutcheoned mantle flowed,
O'er the chained mail, which tinkled as he rode.
The barred vizor raised, you might discern
His clime-changed countenance, though pale, yet stern,
And resolute as death,—whilst in his eye
Sat proud Assurance, Fame, and Victory.

Lautaro, now in manhood's rising pride,
Rode, with a lance, attendant at his side,
In Spanish mantle gracefully arrayed;
Upon his brow a tuft of feathers played:
His glossy locks, with dark and mantling grace,
Shaded the noonday sunbeams on his face.
Though passed in tears the dayspring of his youth,
Valdivia loved his gratitude and truth:
He, in Valdivia, owned a nobler friend;
Kind to protect, and mighty to defend.
So, on he rode; upon his youthful mien
A mild but sad intelligence was seen;
Courage was on his open brow, yet care
Seemed like a wandering shade to linger there;
And though his eye shone, as the eagle's, bright,
It beamed with humid, melancholy light

When now Valdivia saw the embattled line,
Helmets, and swords, and shields, and matchlocks, shine;
Now the long phalanx still and steady stand,
Fixed every eye, and motionless each hand;
Then slowly clustering, into columns wheel,
Each with the red-cross banners of Castile;
While trumps, and drums, and cymbals, to his ear
Made music such as soldiers love to hear;
While horsemen checked their steeds, or, bending low
With levelled lances, o'er the saddle-bow,
Rode gallantly at tilt; and thunders broke,
Instant involving van and rear in smoke,
Till winds the obscuring volume rolled away,
And the red file, stretched out in long array,
More radiant moved beneath the beams of day;
While ensigns, arms, and crosses, glittered bright,—
Philip! he cried, seest thou the glorious sight?
And dost thou deem the tribes of this poor land
Can men, and arms, and steeds, like these, withstand?

Forgive!—the youth replied, and checked a tear,—
The land where my forefathers sleep is dear!—
My native land!—this spot of blessed earth,

The scene where I, and all I love, had birth!
What gratitude fidelity can give
Is yours, my lord!—you shielded—bade me live,
When, in the circuit of the world so wide,
I had but one, one only friend beside.
I bowed resigned to fate; I kissed the hand,
Red with the best blood of my father's land!
But mighty as thou art, Valdivia, know,
Though Cortes' desolating march laid low
The shrines of rich, voluptuous Mexico;
With carcases, though proud Pizarro strew
The Sun's imperial temple in Peru,
Yet the rude dwellers of this land are brave,
And the last spot they lose will be their grave!

A moment's crimson crossed Valdivia's cheek—
Then o'er the plain he spurred, nor deigned to speak,
Waving the youth, at distance, to retire;
None saw the eye that shot terrific fire.
As their commander sternly rode along,
Troop after troop, halted the martial throng;
And all the pennoned trumps a louder blast
Blew, as the Southern World's great victor passed.

Lautaro turned, scarce heeding, from the view,
And from the noise of trumps and drums withdrew;
And now, while troubled thoughts his bosom swell,
Seeks the gray Missionary's humble cell.

Fronting the ocean, but beyond the ken
Of public view, and sounds of murmuring men,
Of unhewn roots composed, and gnarled wood,
A small and rustic oratory stood;
Upon its roof of reeds appeared a cross,
The porch within was lined with mantling moss;
A crucifix and hour-glass, on each side—
One to admonish seemed, and one to guide;
This, to impress how soon life's race is o'er;
And that, to lift our hopes where time shall be no more.
O'er the rude porch, with wild and gadding stray,
The clustering copu weaved its trellis gay;
Two mossy pines, high bending, interwove
Their aged and fantastic arms above.
In front, amid the gay surrounding flowers,
A dial counted the departing hours,
On which the sweetest light of summer shone,—
A rude and brief inscription marked the stone:

To count, with passing shade, the hours,
I placed the dial 'mid the flowers;
That, one by one, came forth, and died,
Blooming, and withering, round its side.
Mortal, let the sight impart
Its pensive moral to thy heart!
Just heard to trickle through a covert near,
And soothing, with perpetual lapse, the ear,
A fount, like rain-drops, filtered through the stone,
And, bright as amber, on the shallows shone.
Intent his fairy pastime to pursue,
And, gem-like, hovering o'er the violets blue,
The humming-bird, here, its unceasing song
Heedlessly murmured, all the summer long;
And when the winter came, retired to rest,
And from the myrtles hung its trembling nest.
No sounds of a conflicting world were near;
The noise of ocean faintly met the ear,
That seemed, as sunk to rest the noontide blast,
But dying sounds of passions that were past;
Or closing anthems, when, far off, expire
The lessening echoes of the distant choir.

Here, every human sorrow hushed to rest,
His pale hands meekly crossed upon his breast,
Anselmo sat: the sun, with westering ray,
Just touched his temples, and his locks of gray.
There was no worldly feeling in his eye;
The world to him was "as a thing gone by."

Now, all his features lit, he raised his look,
Then bent it thoughtful, and unclasped the book;
And whilst the hour-glass shed its silent sand,
A tame opossum licked his withered hand.
That sweetest light of slow-declining day,
Which through the trellis poured its slanting ray,
Resting a moment on his few gray hairs,
Seemed light from heaven sent down to bless his prayers.

When the trump echoed to the quiet spot,
He thought upon the world, but mourned it not;
Enough if his meek wisdom could control,
And bend to mercy, one proud soldier's soul;
Enough, if, while these distant scenes he trod,
He led one erring Indian to his God.

Whence comes my son? with kind complacent look
He asked, and closed again the embossed book.

I come to thee for peace, the youth replied:
Oh, there is strife, and cruelty, and pride,
In this sad Christian world! My native land
Was happy, ere the soldier, with his band
Of fell destroyers, like a vulture, came,
And gave its peaceful scenes to blood and flame.
When will the turmoil of earth's tempests cease?
Father, I come to thee for peace—for peace!

Seek peace, the father cried, with God above:
In His good time, all will be peace and love.
We mourn, indeed, mourn that all sounds of ill,
Earth's fairest scenes with one deep murmur fill;
That yonder sun, when evening paints the sky,
Sinks, beauteous, on a world of misery;
The course of wide destruction to withstand,
We lift our feeble voice—our trembling hand;
But still, bowed low, or smitten to the dust,
Father of mercy, still in Thee we trust!
Through good or ill, in poverty or wealth,
In joy or woe, in sickness or in health,
Meek Piety thy awful hand surveys,
And the faint murmur turns to prayer and praise!
We know—whatever evils we deplore—
Thou hast permitted, and we know no more!
Behold, illustrious on the subject plain,
Some tow'r-crowned city of imperial Spain!
Hark! 'twas the earthquake! clouds of dust alone
Ascend from earth, where tower and temple shone!
Such is the conqueror's dread path: the grave
Yawns for its millions where his banners wave;
But shall vain man, whose life is but a sigh,
With sullen acquiescence gaze and die?
Alas, how little of the mighty maze
Of Providence our mortal ken surveys!
Heaven's awful Lord, pavilioned in the clouds,
Looks through the darkness that all nature shrouds;
And, far beyond the tempest and the night,
Bids man his course hold on to scenes of endless light.

NOTES

The city Baldivia.

He had served in the wars of Italy.

Lautaro had been baptized by that name.

Valdivia had before been in Chili.

A small and beautiful species, which is domesticated.

No part of the world is so subject to earthquakes as Peru.

CANTO THIRD

ARGUMENT

Evening and Night of the same Day

Anselmo's story—Converted Indians—Confession of the Wandering   Minstrel—Night-Scene

Come,—for the sun yet hangs above the bay,—
And whilst our time may brook a brief delay
With other thoughts, and, haply with a tear,
An old man's tale of sorrow thou shalt hear.
I wished not to reveal it;—thoughts that dwell
Deep in the lonely bosom's inmost cell
Unnoticed, and unknown, too painful wake,
And, like a tempest, the dark spirit shake,
When, starting from our slumberous apathy,
We gaze upon the scenes of days gone by.
Yet, if a moment's irritating flush,
Darkens thy cheek, as thoughts conflicting rush,
When I disclose my hidden griefs, the tale
May more than wisdom or reproof prevail.
Oh, may it teach thee, till all trials cease,
To hold thy course, though sorrowing, yet in peace;
Still looking up to Him, the soul's best stay,
Who Faith and Hope shall crown, when worlds are swept away!

Where fair Seville's Morisco turrets gleam
On Guadilquiver's gently-stealing stream;
Whose silent waters, seaward as they glide,
Reflect the wild-rose thickets on its side,
My youth was passed. Oh, days for ever gone!
How touched with Heaven's own light your mornings shone.

Even now, when lonely and forlorn I bend,
My weary journey hastening to its end,
A drooping exile on a distant shore,
I mourn the hours of youth that are no more.
The tender thought amid my prayers has part,

And steals, at times, from Heaven my aged heart.

Forgive the cause, O God!—forgive the tear,
That flows, even now, o'er Leonora's bier;
For, 'midst the innocent and lovely, none
More beautiful than Leonora shone.

As by her widowed mother's side she knelt,
A sad and sacred sympathy I felt.
At Easter-tide, when the high mass was sung,
And, fuming high, the silver censer swung;
When rich-hued windows, from the arches' height,
Poured o'er the shrines a soft and yellow light;
From aisle to aisle, amid the service clear,
When "Adoremus" swelled upon the ear.
(Such as to Heaven thy rapt attention drew
First in the Christian churches of Peru),
She seemed, methought, some spirit of the sky,
Descending to that holy harmony.

But wherefore tell, when life and hope were new,
How by degrees the soul's first passion grew!
I loved her, and I won her virgin heart;
But fortune whispered, we a while must part.

The minster tolled the middle hour of night,
When, waked to agony and wild affright,
I heard those words, words of appalling dread—
"The Holy Inquisition!"—from the bed
I started; snatched my dagger, and my cloak—
Who dare accuse me!—none, in answer, spoke.
The demons seized, in silence, on their prey,
And tore me from my dreams of bliss away.
How frightful was their silence, and their shade,
In torch-light, as their victim they conveyed,
By dark-inscribed, and massy-windowed walls,
Through the dim twilight of terrific halls;
(For thou hast heard me speak of that foul stain
Of pure religion, and the rights of Spain;)
Whilst the high windows shook to night's cold blast,
And echoed to the foot-fall as we passed!

They left me, faint and breathless with affright,
In a cold cell, to solitude and night;
Oh! think, what horror through the heart must thrill
When the last bolt was barred, and all at once was still!

Nor day nor night was here, but a deep gloom,

Sadder than darkness, wrapped the living tomb.
Some bread and water, nature to sustain,
Duly was brought when eve returned again;
And thus I knew, hoping it were the last,
Another day of lingering life was passed.

Five years immured in that deep den of night,
I never saw the sweet sun's blessed light.
Once as the grate, with sullen sound, was barred,
And to the bolts the inmost cavern jarred,
Methought I heard, as clanged the iron door,
A dull and hollow echo from the floor;
I stamped; the vault, and winding caves around,
Returned a long and melancholy sound.
With patient toil I raised a massy stone,
And looked into a depth of shade unknown;
The murky twilight of the lurid place
Helped me, at length, a secret way to trace:
I entered; step by step explored the road,
In darkness, from my desolate abode;
Till, winding through long passages of night,
I saw, at distance, a dim streak of light:—
It was the sun—the bright, the blessed beam
Of day! I knelt—I wept;—the glittering stream
Rolled on beneath me, as I left the cave,
Concealed in woods above the winding wave.

I rested on a verdant bank a while,
I saw around the summer landscape smile;
I gained a peasant's hut; nor dared to leave,
Till, with slow step, advanced the glimmering eve.
Remembering still affection's fondest hours,
I turned my footsteps to the city towers;
In pilgrim's dress, I traced the streets unknown:
No light in Leonora's lattice shone.

The morning came; the busy tumult swells;
Knolling to church, I heard the minster bells;
Involuntary to that scene I strayed,
Disguised, where first I saw my faithful maid.
I saw her, pallid, at the altar stand,
And yield, half-shrinking, her reluctant hand;
She turned her head; she saw my hollow eyes,
And knew me, wasted, wan, in my disguise;
She shrieked, and fell;—breathless, I left the fane
In agony—nor saw her form again;
And from that day her voice, her look were given,
Her name, her memory, to the winds of heaven.

Far off I bent my melancholy way,
Heart-sick and faint, and, in this gown of gray,
From every human eye my sorrows hid,
Unknown, amidst the tumult of Madrid.
Grief in my heart, despair upon my look,
With no companion save my beads and book,
My morsel with Affliction's sons to share,
To tend the sick and poor, my only care,
Forgotten, thus I lived; till day by day
Had worn nigh thirteen years of grief away.

One winter's night, when I had closed my cell,
And bid the labours of the day farewell,
An aged crone approached, with panting breath,
And bade me hasten to the house of death.

I came. With moving lips intent to pray,
A dying woman on a pallet lay;
Her lifted hands were wasted to the bone,
And ghastly on her look the lamp-light shone;
Beside the bed a pious daughter stands
Silent, and, weeping, kisses her pale hands.
Feebly she spoke, and raised her languid head,
Forgive, forgive!—they told me he was dead!—
But in the sunshine of that dreadful day,
That gave me to another's arms away,
I saw him, like a ghost, with deadly stare;
I saw his wasted eye-balls' ghastly glare;
I saw his lips (oh, hide them, God of love!)
I saw his livid lips, half-muttering, move,
To curse the maid—forgetful of her vow:—
Perhaps he lives to curse—to curse me now!

He lives to bless! I cried; and, drawing nigh,
Held up the crucifix; her heavy eye
She raised, and scarce pronounced—Does he yet live?
Can he his lost, his dying child forgive?
Will God forgive—the Lord who bled—will He?—
Ah, no, there is no mercy left for me!

Words were but vain, and colours all too faint,
That awful moment of despair to paint.
She knew me; her exhausted breath, with pain,
Drawing, she pressed my hand, and spoke again:

By a false guardian's cruel wiles deceived,
The tale of fraudful falsehood I believed,

And thought thee dead; he gave the stern command,
And bade me take the rich Antonio's hand.
I knelt, implored, embraced my guardian's knees;
Ruthless inquisitor, he held the keys
Of the dark torture-house. Trembling for life,
Yes, I became a sad, heart-broken wife!
Yet curse me not; of every human care
Already my full heart has had its share:
Abandoned, left in youth to want and woe,
Oh! let these tears, that agonising flow,
Witness how deep ev'n now my heart is rent!
Yet one is lovely—one is innocent!
Protect, protect, (and faint in death she smiled)
When I am dead, protect my orphan child!

The dreadful prison, that so long detained
My wasting life, her dying words explained.
The wretched priest, who wounded me by stealth,
Bartered her love, her innocence for wealth!

I laid her bones in earth; the chanted hymn
Echoed along the hollow cloister dim;
I heard, far off, the bell funereal toll,
And sorrowing said: Now peace be with her soul!

Far o'er the Western Ocean I conveyed,
And Indiana called the orphan maid;
Beneath my eye she grew, and, day by day,
Seemed, grateful, every kindness to repay.

Renouncing Spain, her cruelties and crimes,
Amid untutored tribes, in distant climes,
'Twas mine to spread the light of truth, or save
From stripes and torture the poor Indian slave.
I saw thee, young and innocent, alone,
Cast on the mercies of a race unknown;
I saw, in dark adversity's cold hour,
Thy virtues blooming, like a winter's flower;
From chains and slavery I redeemed thy youth,
Poured on thy mental sight the beams of truth;
By thy warm heart and mild demeanour won,
Called thee my other child—my age's son.
I need not tell the sequel;—not unmoved
Poor Indiana heard thy tale, and loved;
Some sympathy a kindred fate might claim;
Your years, your fortunes, and your friend the same;
Both early of a parent's care bereft,
Both strangers in a world of sadness left;

I marked each slowly-struggling thought; I shed
A tear of love paternal on each head;
And, while I saw her timid eyes incline,
Blessed the affection that had made her thine!
Here let the murmurs of despondence cease:
There is a God—believe—and part in peace!

Rich hues illumed the track of dying day
As the great sun sank in the western bay,
And only its last light yet lingering shone,
Upon the highest palm-tree's feathery cone;
When at a distance on the dewy plain,
In mingled group appeared an Indian train;
Men, women, children, round Anselmo press,
Farewell! they cried. He raised his hand to bless,
And said: My children, may the God above
Still lead you in the paths of peace and love;
To-morrow, we must part;—when I am gone,
Raise on this spot a cross, and place a stone,
That tribes unborn may some memorial have,
When I far off am mouldering in the grave,
Of that poor messenger, who tidings bore
Of Gospel-mercy to your distant shore.

The crowd retired; along the twilight gray,
The condor kept its solitary way,
The fire-flies shone, when to the hermit's cell
Who hastens but the minstrel Zarinel!
In foreign lands, far from his native home,
'Twas his, a gay, romantic youth, to roam,
With a light cittern o'er his shoulders slung,
Where'er he passed he played, and loved, and sung;
And thus accomplished, late had joined the train
Of gallant soldiers on the southern plain.
Father, he cried, uncertain of the fate
That may to-morrow's toilsome march await,
For long will be the road, I would confess
Some secret thoughts that on my bosom press.
They are of one I left, an Indian maid,
Whose trusting love my careless heart betrayed.
Say, may I speak?

Say on, the father cried,
Nor be to penitence all hope denied.
Then hear, Anselmo! From a very child
I loved all fancies marvellous and wild;
I turned from truth, to listen to the lore
Of many an old and fabling troubadour.

Thus, with impassioned heart, and wayward mind,
To dreams and shapes of shadowy things resigned,
I left my native vales and village home,
Wide o'er the world a minstrel boy to roam.

I never shall forget the day, the hour,
When, all my soul resigned to Fancy's power,
First, from the snowy Pyrenees, I cast
My labouring vision o'er the landscape vast,
And saw beneath my feet long vapours float,
Streams, mountains, woods, and ocean's mist remote.
There once I met a soldier, poor and old,
Who tales of Cortes and Bilboa told,
And this new world; he spoke of Indian maids,
Rivers like seas, and forests whose deep shades
Had never yet been pierced by morning ray,
And how the green bird mocked, and talked all day.

Imagination thus, in colours new,
This distant world presented to my view;
Young, and enchanted with the fancied scene,
I crossed the toiling seas that roared between,
And with ideal images impressed,
Stood on these unknown shores a wondering guest.

Still to romantic phantasies resigned,
I left Callao's crowded port behind,
And climbed the mountains which their shadow threw
Upon the lessening summits of Peru.
Some sheep the armed peasants drove before,
That all our food through the wild passes bore,
Had wandered in the frost-smoke of the morn,
Far from the track; I blew the signal horn—
But echo only answered: 'mid the snows,
Wildered and lost, I saw the evening close.
The sun was setting in the crimson west;
In all the earth I had no home of rest;
The last sad light upon the ice-hills shone;
I seemed forsaken in a world unknown;
How did my cold and sinking heart rejoice,
When, hark! methought I heard a human voice!
It might be some wild Indian's roving troop,
Or the dread echo of their distant whoop;
Still it was human, and I seemed to find
Again some commerce with remote mankind.
The voice comes nearer, rising through the shade—
Is it the song of some rude mountain-maid?
And now I heard the tread of hastening feet,

And, in the western glen, a Llama bleat.
I listened—all is still; but hark! again
Near and more near is heard the welcome strain;
It is a wild maid's carolling, who seeks
Her wandering Llama 'midst the snowy peaks:
Truant, she cried, thy lurking place is found!

With languid touch I waked the cittern's sound,
And soon a maid, by the pale light, I saw
Gaze breathless with astonishment and awe:
What instant terrors to her fancy rose,
Ha! is it not the Spirit of the snows!
But when she saw me, weary, cold, and weak,
Stretch forth my hand (for now I could not speak),
She pitied, raised me from the snows, and led
My faltering footsteps to her father's shed;
The Llama followed with her tinkling bell;
The dwelling rose within a craggy dell,
O'erhung with icy summits. To be brief,
She was the daughter of an aged chief;
He, by her gentle voice to pity won,
Showed mercy, for himself had lost a son.
The father spoke not; by the pine-wood blaze,
The daughter stood, and turned a cake of maize;
And then, as sudden shone the light, I saw
Such features as no artist hand might draw.
Her form, her face, her symmetry, her air,
Father! thy age must such recital spare:—
She saved my life; and kindness, if not love,
Might sure in time the coldest bosom move!
Mine was not cold; she loved to hear me sing,
And sometimes touched with playful hand the string;
And when I waked some melancholy strain,
She wept, and smiled, and bade me sing again.
So many a happy day, in this deep glen,
Far from the noise of life, and sounds of men,
Was passed! Nay, father, the sad sequel hear:
'Twas now the leafy spring-time of the year—
Ambition called me: true, I knew to part
Would break her generous, warm, and trusting heart;
True, I had vowed, but now estranged and cold,
She saw my look, and shuddered to behold:—
She would go with me, leave the lonely glade
Where she grew up, but my stern voice forbade;
She hid her face and wept: Go then away,
(Father, methinks, ev'n now, I hear her say)
Go to thy distant land, forget this tear,
Forget these rocks, forget I once was dear;

Fly to the world, o'er the wide ocean fly,
And leave me unremembered here to die!
Yet to my father should I all relate,
Death, instant death, would be a traitor's fate!

Nor fear, nor pity moved my stubborn mind,
I left her sorrows and the scene behind;
I sought Valdivia on the southern plain,
And joined the careless military train;
Oh! ere I sleep, thus, lowly on my knee,
Father, I absolution crave from thee!

Anselmo spoke, with look and voice severe:
Yes, thoughtless youth, my absolution hear.
First, by deep penitence the wrong atone,
Then absolution ask from God alone!
Yet stay, and to my warning voice attend,
And hear me as a father, and a friend.
Let Truth severe be wayward Fancy's guide,
Let stern-eyed Conscience o'er each thought preside;
The passions, that on noblest natures prey,
Oh! cast them, like corroding bonds, away!
Disdain to act mean falsehood's coward part,
And let religion dignify thine art.
If, by thy bed, thou seest at midnight stand
Pale Conscience, pointing, with terrific hand,
To deeds of darkness done, whilst, like a corse,
To shake thy soul, uprises dire Remorse;
Fly to God's mercy, fly, ere yet too late—
Perhaps one hour marks thy eternal fate;
Let the warm tear of deep contrition flow,
The heart obdurate melt, like softening snow,
The last vain follies of thy youth deplore,
Then go, in secret weep, and sin no more!

The stars innumerous in their watches shone—
Anselmo knelt before the cross alone.
Ten thousand glowing orbs their pomp displayed,
Whilst, looking up, thus silently he prayed:—

Oh! how oppressive to the aching sense,
How fearful were this vast magnificence,
This prodigality of glory, spread
Above a poor and dying emmet's head,
That toiled his transient hour upon the shore
Of mortal life, and then was seen no more;
If man beheld, on his terrific throne,
A dark, cold, distant Deity, alone!

Felt no relating, no endearing tie,
That Hope might upwards raise her glistening eye,
And think, with deep unutterable bliss,
In yonder radiant realm my kingdom is!

More glorious than those orbs that silent roll,
Shines Heaven's redeeming mercy on the soul—
Oh, pure effulgence of unbounded love!
In Thee, I think—I feel—I live—I move;
Yet when, O Thou, whose name is Love and Light,
When will thy Dayspring on these realms of night
Arise! Oh! when shall severed nations raise
One hallelujah of triumphant praise,
Tibet on Fars, Andes on Atlas call,
And "roll the loud hosannah" round the ball!

Soon may Thy kingdom come, that love, and peace,
And charity, may bid earth's chidings cease!
Meantime, in life or death, through good or ill,
Thy poor and feeble servant, I fulfil,
As best I may, Thy high and holy will,
Till, weary, on the world my eyelids close,
And I enjoy my long and last repose!

NOTES

Indians of Chili are of the lightest class, called by some "white Indians."

—Of Moorish architecture.

Seville was the first place in Spain in which the Inquisition was established, in.

CANTO FOURTH

ARGUMENT

Assembly of Indian warriors—Caupolican, Ongolmo, Teucapel, Mountain-chief—Song of the Indian Wizard—White woman and child

Far in the centre of the deepest wood,
The assembled fathers of their country stood.
'Twas midnight now; the pine-wood fire burned red,
And to the leaves a shadowy glimmer spread;
The struggling smoke, or flame with fitful glance,
Obscured, or showed, some dreadful countenance;

And every warrior, as his club he reared,
With larger shadow, indistinct, appeared;
While more terrific, his wild locks and mien,
And fierce eye, through the quivering smoke, was seen.

In sea-wolf's skin, here Mariantu stood;
Gnashed his white teeth, impatient, and cried, blood!
His lofty brow, with crimson feathers bound,
Here, brooding death, the huge Ongolmo frowned;
And, like a giant of no earthly race,
To his broad shoulders heaved his ponderous mace.
With lifted hatchet, as in act to fell,
Here stood the young and ardent Teucapel.
Like a lone cypress, stately in decay,
When time has worn its summer boughs away,
And hung its trunk with moss and lichens sere,
The Mountain-warrior rested on his spear.
And thus, and at this hour, a hundred chiefs,
Chosen avengers of their country's griefs;
Chiefs of the scattered tribes that roam the plain,
That sweeps from Andes to the western main,
Their country-gods, around the coiling smoke,
With sacrifice, and silent prayers, invoke.
For all, at first, were silent as the dead;
The pine was heard to whisper o'er their head,
So stood the stern assembly; but apart,
Wrapped in the spirit of his fearful art,
Alone, to hollow sounds of hideous hum,
The wizard-seer struck his prophetic drum.

Silent they stood, and watched with anxious eyes,
What phantom-shape might from the ground arise;
No voices came, no spectre-form appeared;
A hollow sound, but not of winds, was heard
Among the leaves, and distant thunder low,
Which seemed like moans of an expiring foe.
His crimson feathers quivering in the smoke,
Then, with loud voice, first Mariantu spoke:

Hail we the omen! Spirits of the slain,
I hear your voices! Mourn, devoted Spain!
Pale-visaged tyrants! still, along our coasts,
Shall we despairing mark your iron hosts!
Spirits of our brave fathers, curse the race
Who thus your name, your memory disgrace!
No; though yon mountain's everlasting snows
In vain Almagro's toilsome march oppose;
Though Atacama's long and wasteful plain

Be heaped with blackening carcases in vain;
Though still fresh hosts those snowy summits scale,
And scare the Llamas with their glittering mail;
Though sullen castles lour along our shore;
Though our polluted soil be drenched with gore;
Insolent tyrants! we, prepared to die,
Your arms, your horses, and your gods, defy!

He spoke: the warriors stamped upon the ground,
And tore the feathers that their foreheads bound.
Insolent tyrants! burst the general cry,
We, met for vengeance—we, prepared to die,
Your arms, your horses, and your gods, defy!

Then Teucapel, with warm emotion, cried:
This hatchet never yet in blood was dyed;
May it be buried deep within my heart,
If living from the conflict I depart,
Till loud, from shore to shore, is heard one cry,
See! in their gore where the last tyrants lie!

The Mountain-warrior: Oh, that I could raise
The hatchet too, as in my better days,
When victor on Maypocha's banks I stood;
And while the indignant river rolled in blood,
And our swift arrows hissed like rushing rain,
I cleft Almagro's iron helm in twain!
My strength is well-nigh gone! years marked with woe
Have o'er me passed, and bowed my spirit low!
Alas, I have no son! Beloved boy,
Thy father's last, best hope, his pride, his joy!
Oh, hadst thou lived, sole object of my prayers,
To guard my waning life, and these gray hairs,
How bravely hadst thou now, in manhood's pride,
Swung the uplifted war-club by my side!
But the Great Spirit willed not! Thou art gone;
And, weary, on this earth I walk alone;
Thankful if I may yield my latest breath,
And bless my country in the pangs of death!

With words deliberate, and uplifted hand,
Mild to persuade, yet dauntless to command,
Raising his hatchet high, Caupolican
Surveyed the assembled chiefs, and thus began:

Friends, fathers, brothers, dear and sacred names!
Your stern resolve each ardent look proclaims;
On then to conquest; let one hope inspire,

One spirit animate, one vengeance fire!
Who doubts the glorious issue! To our foes
A tenfold strength and spirit we oppose.
In them no god protects his mortal sons,
Or speaks, in thunder, from their roaring guns.
Nor come they children of the radiant sky;
But, like the wounded snake, to writhe and die.
Then, rush resistless on their prostrate bands,
Snatch the red lightning from their feeble hands,
And swear to the great spirits, hovering near,
Who now this awful invocation hear,
That we shall never see our household hearth,
Till, like the dust, we sweep them from the earth.
But vain our strength, that idly, in the fight,
Tumultuous wastes its ineffectual might,
Unless to one the hatchet we confide;
Let one our numbers, one our counsels guide.
And, lo! for all that in this world is dear,
I raise this hatchet, raise it high, and swear,
Never again to lay it down, till we,
And all who love this injured land, are free!

At once the loud acclaim tumultuous ran:
Our spears, our life-blood, for Caupolican!
With thee, for all that in this world is dear,
We lift our hatchets, lift them high, and swear,
Never again to lay them down, till we,
And all who love this injured land, are free!

Then thus the chosen chief: Bring forth the slave,
And let the death-dance recreate the brave.

Two warriors led a Spanish captive, bound
With thongs; his eyes were fixed upon the ground.
Dark cypresses the mournful spot inclose:
High in the midst an ancient mound arose,
Marked on each side with monumental stones,
And white beneath with skulls and scattered bones.
Four poniards, on the mound, encircling stood,
With points erect, dark with forgotten blood.

Forthwith, with louder voice, the chief commands:
Bring forth the lots, unbind the captive's hands;
Then north, towards his country, turn his face,
And dig beneath his feet a narrow space.

Caupolican uplifts his axe, and cries:
Gods, of our land be yours this sacrifice!—

Now, listen, warriors!—and forthwith commands
To place the billets in the captive's hands—
Soldier, cast in the lot!

With looks aghast,
The captive in the trench a billet cast.
Soldier, declare, who leads the arms of Spain,
Where Santiago frowns upon the plain?

CAPTIVE
Villagra!

WARRIOR
Earth upon the billet heap;
So may a tyrant's heart be buried deep!
The dark woods echoed to the long acclaim,
Accursed be his nation and his name!

WARRIOR
Captive, declare who leads the Spanish bands,
Where the proud fortress shades Coquimbo's sands.

CAPTIVE
Ocampo!

WARRIOR
Earth upon the billet heap;
So may a tyrant's heart be buried deep!
The dark woods echoed to the long acclaim,
Accursed be his nation and his name!

WARRIOR
Cast in the lot.

Again, with looks aghast,
The captive in the trench a billet cast.
Pronounce his name who here pollutes the plain,
The leader of the mailed hosts of Spain!

CAPTIVE
Valdivia!

At that name a sudden cry
Burst forth, and every lance was lifted high.

WARRIOR
Valdivia!

Earth upon the billet heap;
So may a tyrant's heart be buried deep!
The dark woods echoed to the long acclaim,
Accursed be his nation and his name!

And now loud yells, and whoops of death resound;
The shuddering captive ghastly gazed around,
When the huge war-club smote him to the ground.
Again deep stillness hushed the listening crowd,
While the prophetic wizard sang aloud.

SONG TO THE GOD OF WAR

By thy habitation dread,
In the valley of the dead,
Where no sun, nor day, nor night,
Breaks the red and dusky light;
By the grisly troops, that ride,
Of slaughtered Spaniards, at thy side,—
Slaughtered by the Indian spear,
Mighty Epananum, hear!
Hark, the battle! Hark, the din!
Now the deeds of Death begin!
The Spaniards come, in clouds! above,
I hear their hoarse artillery move!
Spirits of our fathers slain,
Haste, pursue the dogs of Spain!
The noise was in the northern sky!
Haste, pursue! They fly—they fly!
Now from the cavern's secret cell,
Where the direst phantoms dwell,
See they rush, and, riding high,
Break the moonlight as they fly;
And, on the shadowed plain beneath,
Shoot, unseen, the shafts of Death!
O'er the devoted Spanish camp,
Like a vapour, dark and damp,
May they hover, till the plain
Is hid beneath the countless slain;
And none but silent women tread
From corse to corse, to seek the dead!

The wavering fire flashed with expiring light,
When shrill and hollow, through the cope of night,
A distant shout was heard; at intervals,
Increasing on the listening ear it falls.
It ceased; when, bursting from the thickest wood,

With lifted axe, two gloomy warriors stood;
Wan in the midst, with dark and streaming hair,
Blown by the winds upon her bosom bare,
A woman, faint from terror's wild alarms,
And folding a white infant in her arms,
Appeared. Each warrior stooped his lance to gaze
On her pale looks, seen ghastlier through the blaze.
Save! she exclaimed, with harrowed aspect wild;
Oh, save my innocent, my helpless child!
Then fainting fell, as from death's instant stroke;
Caupolican, with stern inquiry, spoke:
Whence come, to interrupt our awful rite,
At this dread hour, the warriors of the night?

From ocean.

Who is she who fainting lies,
And now scarce lifts her supplicating eyes?

The Spanish ship went down; the seamen bore,
In a small boat, this woman to the shore:
They fell beneath our hatchets,—and again,
We gave them back to the insulted main.
The child and woman—of a race we hate—
Warriors, 'tis yours, here to decide their fate.

Vengeance! aloud fierce Mariantu cried:
Let vengeance on the race be satisfied!
Let none of hated Spanish blood remain,
Woman or child, to violate our plain!

Amid that dark and bloody scene, the child
Stretched to the mountain-chief his hands and smiled.
A starting tear of pity dimmed the eye
Of the old warrior, though he knew not why.
Oh, think upon your little ones! he cried,
Nor be compassion to the weak denied.

Caupolican then fixed his aspect mild
On the white woman and her shrinking child,
Then firmly spoke:—

White woman, we were free,
When first thy brethren of the distant sea
Came to our shores! White woman, theirs the guilt!
Theirs, if the blood of innocence be spilt!
Yet blood we seek not, though our arms oppose
The hate of foreign and remorseless foes;

Thou camest here a captive, so abide,
Till the Great Spirit shall our cause decide.
He spoke: the warriors of the night obey;
And, ere the earliest streak of dawning day,
They lead her from the scene of blood away.

NOTES

The first Spaniard who visited Chili. He entered it by the dreadful passage of the snows of the Andes; but afterwards the passage was attempted through the desert of Atacama.

The reader is referred to Molina for a particular description of the war sacrifice, which is very striking and poetical.

Name of the War-deity.

Terrific imaginary beings, called "man-animals," that leave their caves by night, and scatter pestilence and death as they fly.—See Molina.

"Render them back upon the insulted ocean."—Coleridge.

CANTO FIFTH

ARGUMENT

Ocean Cave—Spanish Captive—Wild Indian Maid—Genius of Andes, and Spirits

'Tis dawn:—the distant Andes' rocky spires,
One after one, have caught the orient fires.
Where the dun condor shoots his upward flight,
His wings are touched with momentary light.
Meantime, beneath the mountains' glittering heads,
A boundless ocean of gray vapour spreads,
That o'er the champaign, stretching far below,
Moves now, in clustered masses, rising slow,
Till all the living landscape is displayed
In various pomp of colour, light, and shade,
Hills, forests, rivers, lakes, and level plain,
Lessening in sunshine to the southern main.
The Llama's fleece fumes with ascending dew;
The gem-like humming-birds their toils renew;
And there, by the wild river's devious side,
The tall flamingo, in its crimson pride,
Stalks on, in richest plumage bright arrayed,
With snowy neck superb, and legs of lengthening shade.

Sad maid, for others may the valleys ring,
For other ears the birds of morning sing;
For other eyes the palms in beauty wave,
Dark is thy prison in the ocean-cave!

Amid that winding cavern's inmost shade,
A dripping rill its ceaseless murmur made:
Masses of dim-discovered crags aloof,
Hung, threatening, from the vast and vaulted roof:
And through a fissure, in its glimmering height,
Seen like a star, appeared the distant light;
Beneath the opening, where the sunbeams shine,
Far down, the rock-weed hung its slender twine.

Here, pale and bound, the Spanish captive lay,
Till morn on morn, in silence, passed away;
When once, as o'er her sleeping child she hung,
And sad her evening supplication sung;
Like a small gem, amidst the gloom of night,
A glow-worm shot its green and trembling light,—
And, 'mid the moss and craggy fragments, shed
Faint lustre o'er her sleeping infant's head;
And hark! a voice—a woman's voice, its sound
Dies in faint echoes, 'mid the vault profound:

Let us pity the poor white maid!
She has no mother near!
No friend to dry her tear!
Upon the cold earth she is laid:
Let us pity the poor white maid!

It seemed the burden of a song of woe;
And see, across the gloom an Indian girl move slow!
Her nearer look is sorrowful, yet mild,
Her hanging locks are wreathed with rock-weed wild;
Gently she spoke, Poor Christian, dry thy tear:
Art thou afraid? all are not cruel here.
Oh! still more wretched may my portion be,
Stranger, if I could injure thine and thee!
And, lo! I bring, from banks and thickets wild,
Wood-strawberries, and honey for thy child.
Whence, who art thou, who, in this fearful place,
Does comfort speak to one of Spanish race?

INDIAN
It is an Indian maid, who chanced to hear
Thy tale of sorrow, as she wandered near:

I loved a white man once; but he is flown,
And now I wander heartless and alone.
I traced the dark and winding way beneath:
But well I know to lead thee hence were death.
Oh, say! what fortunes cast thee o'er the wave,
On these sad shores perhaps to find a grave?

SPANISH WOMAN
Three years have passed since a fond husband left
Me and this infant, of his love bereft;
Him I have followed; need I tell thee more,
Cast helpless, friendless, hopeless, on this shore.

INDIAN
Oh! did he love thee, then? Let death betide,
Yes, from this cavern I will be thy guide.
Nay, do not shrink! from Caracalla's bay,
Ev'n now, the Spaniards wind their march this way.
As late in yester eve I paced the shore
I heard their signal-guns at distance roar.
Wilt thou not follow? He will shield thy child,—
The Christian's God,—through passes dark and wild
He will direct thy way! Come, follow me;
Oh, yet be loved, be happy, and be free!
But I, an outcast on my native plain,
The poor Olola ne'er shall smile again!
So guiding from the cave, when all was still,
And pointing to the furthest glimmering hill,
The Indian led, till, on Itata's side,
The Spanish camp and night-fires they descried:
Then on the stranger's neck that wild maid fell,
And said, Thy own gods prosper thee, farewell!

The owl is hooting overhead; below,
On dusky wing, the vampire-bat sails slow.
Ongolmo stood before the cave of night,
Where the great wizard sat:—a lurid light
Was on his face; twelve giant shadows frowned,
His mute and dreadful ministers, around.
Each eye-ball, as in life, was seen to roll,
Each lip to move; but not a living soul
Was there, save bold Ongolmo and the seer.
The warrior half advanced his lifted spear,
Then spoke: Dread master of the mighty lore!
Say, shall the Spaniards welter in their gore?
Let these dark ministers the answer tell,
Replied the master of the mighty spell.
Then every giant-shadow, as it stood,

Lifted on high a skull that dropped with blood.
Yet more, the impatient warrior cried; yet more!
Say, shall I live, and drink the tyrant's gore?
'Twas silence. Speak! he cried: none made reply.
At once strange thunder shook the distant sky,
And all was o'er; the grisly shapes are flown,
And the grim warrior stands in the wild woods alone.

St Pedro's church had rung its midnight chimes,
And the gray friars were chanting at their primes,
When winds, as of a rushing hurricane,
Shook the tall windows of the towered fane;—
Sounds more than earthly with the storm arose,
And a dire troop are passed to Andes' snows,
Where mighty spirits in mysterious ring
Their dread prophetic incantations sing,
Round Chillan's crater-smoke, whose lurid light
Streams high against the hollow cope of night.
Thy genius, Andes, towering o'er the rest,
Rose vast, and thus a phantom-shape addressed:
Who comes so swift amid the storm?
Ha! I know thy bloodless form,
I know thee, angel, who thou art,
By the hissing of thy dart!
'Tis Death, the king! the rocks around,
Hark! echo back the fearful sound;—
'Tis Death, the king! away, away!
The famished vulture scents its prey.
Spectre, hence! we cannot die—
Thy withering weapons we defy;
Dire and potent as thou art!
Then spoke the phantom of the uplifted dart:
Spirits who in darkness dwell,
I heard far off your secret spell!
Enough, on yonder fatal shore,
My fiends have drank your children's gore;
Lo! I come, and doom to fate
The murderers, and the foe you hate!
Of all who shook their hostile spears,
And marked their way through blood and tears,
(Now sleeping still on yonder plain)
But one—one only shall remain,
Ere thrice the morn shall shine again.

Then sang the mighty spirits. Thee, they sing,
Hail to thee, Death, all hail to Death, the king!
The penguin flaps her wings in gore,
Devoted Spain, along the shore.

Whence that shriek? with ghastly eyes,
Thy victor-chief abandoned lies!
Victor of the southern world,
Whose crimson banners were unfurled
O'er the silence of the waves,—
O'er a land of bleeding slaves!
Victor, where is now thy boast;
Thine iron steeds, thy mailed host?
Hark! hark! even now I hear his cries!—
Spirits, hence!—he dies! he dies!

NOTES

The neck of the flamingo is white, and its wings of rich and beautiful crimson.

From Mungo Park.

The owl is an object of peculiar dread to the Indian of Chili.

CANTO SIXTH

ARGUMENT

The City of Conception—The City of Penco—Castle—Lautaro—Wild Indian Maid—Zarinel—Missionary

The second moon had now begun to wane,
Since bold Valdivia left the southern plain;
Goal of his labours, Penco's port and bay,
Far gleaming to the summer sunset lay.

The wayworn veteran, who had slowly passed
Through trackless woods, or o'er savannahs vast,
With hope impatient sees the city spires
Gild the horizon, like ascending fires.

Now well-known sounds salute him, as more near
The citadel and battlements appear;
The approaching trumpets ring at intervals;
The trumpet answers from the rampart walls,
Where many a maiden casts an anxious eye,
Some long-lost object of her love to espy,
Or watches, as the evening light illumes
The points of lances, or the passing plumes.
The grating drawbridge and the portal-arch,
Now echo to the long battalion's march;

Whilst every eye some friend remembered greets,
Amid the gazing crowd that throngs the streets.

As bending o'er his mule, amid the throng,
Pensive and pale, Anselmo rode along,
How sacred, 'mid the noise of arms, appeared
His venerable mien and snowy beard!
Whilst every heart a silent prayer bestowed,
Slow to the convent's massy gate he rode:
Around, the brothers, gratulating, stand,
And ask for tidings of the southern land.

As from the turret tolls the vesper bell,
He seeks, a weary man, his evening cell,
No sounds of social cheer, no beds of state,
Nor gorgeous canopies his coming wait;
But o'er a little bread, with folded hands,
Thanking the God that gave, a while he stands;
Then, while all thoughts of earthly sorrow cease,
Upon his pallet lays him down in peace.

The scene how different, where the castle-hall
Rings to the loud triumphant festival:
A hundred torches blaze, and flame aloof,
Long quivering shadows streak the vaulted roof,—
Whilst, seen far off, the illumined windows throw
A splendour on the shore and seas below.

Amid his captains, in imperial state,
Beneath a crimson canopy, elate,
Valdivia sits—and, striking loud the strings,
The wandering ministrel of Valentia sings.
For Chili conquered, fill the bowl again!
For Chili conquered, raise the heroic strain!

Lautaro left the hall of jubilee
Unmarked, and wandered by the moonlit sea:
He heard far off, in dissonant acclaim,
The song, the shout, and his loved country's name.
As swelled at times the trump's insulting sound,
He raised his eyes impatient from the ground;
Then smote his breast indignantly, and cried,
Chili! my country; would that I had died
On the sad night of that eventful day
When on the ground my murdered father lay!
I should not then, dejected and alone,
Have thought I heard his injured spirit groan.
Ha! was it not his form—his face—his hair?

Hold, soldier! stern, inhuman soldier, spare!
Ha! is it not his blood? Avenge, he cries,
Avenge, my son, these wounds! He faints—he dies!
Leave me, dread shadow! Can I then forget
My father's look—his voice? He beckons yet!
Now on that glimmering rock I see him stand:
Avenge! he cries, and waves his dim-seen hand!
Thus mused the youth, distempered and forlorn,
When, hark! the sound as of a distant horn
Swells o'er the surge! he turned his look around,
And still, with many a pause, he heard the sound:
It came from yonder rocks; and, list! what strain
Breaks on the silence of the sleeping main?

I heard the song of gladness;
It seemed but yesterday,
But it turned my thoughts to madness,
So soon it died away:
I sound my sea-shell; but in vain I try
To bring back that enchanting harmony!
Hark! heard ye not the surges say,
Oh! heartless maid, what canst thou do?
O'er the moon-gleaming ocean, I'll wander away,
And paddle to Spain in my light canoe!
The youth drew near, by the strange accents led,
Where in a cave, wild sea-weeds round her head,
And holding a large sea-conch in her hand,
He saw, with wildering air, an Indian maiden stand.
A tattered poncho o'er her shoulders hung;
On either side her long black locks were flung;
And now by the moon's glimmer, he espies
Her high cheek-bones, and bright but hollow eyes.
Lautaro spoke: Oh! say what cruel wrong
Weighs on thy heart, maiden, what bodes thy song?
She answered not, but blew her shell again;
Then thus renewed the desultory strain:
Yes, yes, we must forget! the world is wide;
My music now shall be the dashing tide:
In the calm of the deep I will frolic and swim—
With the breath of the South o'er the sea-blossom skim.

If ever, stranger, on thy way,
Sounds, more than earthly sweet, thy soul should move,
It is the youth! Oh! do not say—
That poor Olola died for love.
Lautaro stretched his hand; she said, Adieu!
And o'er the glimmering rocks like lightning flew.
He followed, and still heard at distance swell

The lessening echoes of that mournful shell.
It ceased at once; and now he heard no more
Than the sea's murmur dying on the shore.
Olola!—ha! his sister had that name!
Oh, horrid fancies! shake not thus his frame!
All night he wandered by the desert main,
To catch the melancholy sounds again.

No torches blaze in Penco's castled hall
That echoed to the midnight festival.
The weary soldiers by their toils oppressed,
Had now retired to silence and to rest.
The minstrel only, who the song had sung
Of noble Cid, as o'er the strings he hung,
Upon the instrument had fall'n asleep,
Weary, and now was hushed in slumbers deep.
Tracing the scenes long past, in busy dreams
Again he wanders by his native streams;
Or sits, his evening saraband to sing
To the clear Garonne's gentle murmuring.

Cold o'er the fleckered clouds the morning broke
Aslant ere from his slumbers he awoke;
Still as he sat, nor yet had left the place,
The first dim light fell on his pallid face.
He wakes—he gazes round—the dawning day
Comes from the deep, in garb of cloudy gray.
The woods with crow of early turkeys ring,
The glancing birds beneath the castle sing,
And the sole sun his rising orb displays,
Radiant and reddening, through the scattered haze.

To recreate the languid sense a while,
When earth and ocean wore their sweetest smile,
He wandered to the beach: the early air
Blew soft, and lifted, as it blew, his hair;
Flushed was his cheek; his faded eye, more bright,
Shone with a faint but animated light,
While the soft morning ray seemed to bestow
On his tired mind a transient kindred glow.
As thus, with shadow stretching o'er the sand,
He mused and wandered on the winding strand,
At distance tossed upon the tumbling tide,
A dark and floating substance he espied.
He stood, and where the eddying surges beat,
An Indian corse was rolled beneath his feet:
The hollow wave retired with sullen sound;
The face of that sad corse was to the ground;

It seemed a female, by the slender form;
He touched the hand—it was no longer warm;
He turned its face—O God! that eye, though dim,
Seemed with its deadly glare as fixed on him!
How sunk his shuddering sense, how changed his hue,
When poor Olola in that corse he knew!
Lautaro, rushing from the rocks, advanced;
His keen eye, like a startled eagle's glanced:
'Tis she!—he knew her by a mark impressed
From earliest infancy beneath her breast.

Oh, my poor sister! when all hopes were past
Of meeting, do we meet—thus meet—at last!
Then full on Zarinel, as one amazed,
With rising wrath and stern suspicion gazed;
For Zarinel still knelt upon the sand,
And to his forehead pressed the dead maid's hand.
Speak! whence art thou?

Pale Zarinel, his head
Upraising answered,
Peace is with the dead!
Him dost thou seek who injured thine and thee?
Here—strike the fell assassin—I am he!

Die! he exclaimed, and with convulsive start
Instant had plunged the dagger in his heart,
When the meek father, with his holy book,
And placid aspect, met his frenzied look.
He trembled—struck his brow—and, turning round,
Flung the uplifted dagger to the ground.
Then murmured: Father, Heaven has heard thy prayer—
But oh! the sister of my soul lies there!
The Christian's God has triumphed! father, heap
Some earth upon her bones, whilst I go weep!
Anselmo with calm brow approached the place,
And hastened with his staff his faltering pace:
Ho! child of guilt and wretchedness, he cried,
Speak!—Holy father, the sad youth replied,
God bade the seas the accusing victim roll
Dead at my feet, to teach my shuddering soul
Its guilt: Oh! father, holy father, pray
That heaven may take the deep, dire curse away!

Oh! yet, Anselmo cried, live and repent,
For not in vain was this dread warning sent;
The deep reproaches of thy soul I spare,
Go! seek Heaven's peace by penitence and prayer.

The youth arose, yet trembling from the shock,
And severed from the dead maid's hair a lock;
This to his heart with trembling hand he pressed,
And dried the salt-sea moisture on his breast.
They laid her limbs within the sea-beat grave,
And prayed: Her soul, O blessed Mary, save!

NOTES

The "sea-blossom," Holothuria, known to seamen by the name of "Portuguese man of war," is among the most striking and beautiful objects in the calms of the Southern ocean.

CANTO SEVENTH

ARGUMENT

Midnight—Valdivia's tent—Missionary—March to the Valley Arauco—First sight of assembled Indians.

The watchman on the tower his bugle blew,
And swelling to the morn the streamers flew;
The rampart-guns a dread alarum gave,
Smoke rolled, and thunder echoed o'er the wave;
When, starting from his couch, Valdivia cried,
What tidings? Of the tribes! a scout replied;
Ev'n now, prepared thy bulwarks to assail,
Their gathering numbers darken all the vale!
Valdivia called to the attendant youth,
Philip, he cried, belike thy words have truth;
The formidable host, by holy James,
Might well appal our priests and city dames!
Dost thou not fear? Nay—dost thou not reply?
Now by the rood, and all the saints on high,
I hold it sin that thou shouldst lift thy hand
Against thy brothers in thy native land!
But, as thou saidst, those mighty enemies
Me and my feeble legions would despise.
Yes, by our holy lady, thou shalt ride,
Spectator of their prowess, by my side!
Come life, come death, our battle shall display
Its ensigns to the earliest beam of day!
With louder summons ring the rampart-bell,
And haste the shriving father from his cell;
A soldier's heart rejoices in alarms:
And let the trump at midnight sound to arms!

And now, obedient to the chief's commands,
The gray-haired priest before the soldier stands.
Father, Valdivia cried, fierce are our foes,—
The last event of war GOD only knows;—
Let mass be sung; father, this very night
I would attend the high and holy rite.
Yet deem not that I doubt of victory,
Or place defeat or death before mine eye;
It blenches not! But, whatsoe'er befall,
Good father, I would part in peace with all.
So, tell Lautaro—his ingenuous mind
Perhaps may grieve, if late I seemed unkind:—
Hear my heart speak, though far from virtue's way
Ambition's lure hath led my steps astray,
No wanton exercise of barbarous power
Harrows my shrinking conscience at this hour.
If hasty passions oft my spirit fire,
They flash a moment and the next expire;
Lautaro knows it. There is somewhat more:
I would not, here—here, on this distant shore
(Should they, the Indian multitudes, prevail,
And this good sword and these firm sinews fail)
Amid my deadly enemies be found,
"Unhouseled, ananealed," upon the ground,
A dying man;—thy look, thy reverend age,
Might save my poor remains from barb'rous rage;
And thou may'st pay the last sad obsequies,
O'er the heaped earth where a brave soldier lies:—
So GOD be with thee!

By the torches' light,
The slow procession moves; the solemn rite
Is chanted: through the aisles and arches dim,
At intervals, is heard the imploring hymn.
Now all is still, that only you might hear—
(The tall and slender tapers burning clear,
Whose light Anselmo's palid brow illumes,
Now glances on the mailed soldier's plumes)
Hear, sounding far, only the iron tread,
That echoed through the cloisters of the dead.
Dark clouds are wandering o'er the heaven's wide way;
Now from the camp, at times, a horse's neigh
Breaks on the ear; and on the rampart height
The sentinel proclaims the middle watch of night.
By the dim taper's solitary ray,
Tired, in his tent, the sovereign soldier lay.

Meantime, as shadowy dreams arise, he roams
'Mid bright pavilions and imperial domes,
Where terraces, and battlements, and towers,
Glisten in air o'er rich romantic bowers.
Sudden the visionary pomp is past;
The vacant court sounds to the moaning blast;
A dismal vault appears, where, with swoll'n eyes,
As starting from their orbs, a dead man lies.
It is Almagro's corse!—roll on, ye drums,
Lo! where the great, the proud Pizarro comes!
Her gold, her richest gems, let Fortune strew
Before the mighty conqueror of Peru!
Ah, turn, and see a dagger in his hand—
With ghastly look—see the assassin stand!
Pizarro falls;—he welters in his gore!
Lord of the western world, art thou no more!
Valdivia, hark!—it was another groan!
Another shadow comes, it is thy own!
Ah, bind not thus his arms!—give, give him breath!
Wipe from his bleeding brow those damps of death!

Valdivia, starting, woke. He is alone:
The taper in his tent yet dimly shone.
Lautaro, haste! he cried; Lautaro, save
Thy dying master! Ah! is this the brave,
The haughty victor? Hush, the dream is past!
The early trumpets ring the second blast!
Arm, arm! Ev'n now, the impatient charger neighs!
Again, from tent to tent the trumpet brays!
By torch-light, then, Valdivia gave command,
Haste, let Del Oro take a chosen band,
With watchful caution, on his fleetest steed,
A troop observant on the heights to lead.

Now beautiful, beneath the heaven's gray arch,
Appeared the main battalion's moving march;
The banner of the cross was borne before,
And next, with aspect sad, and tresses hoar,
The holy man went thoughtfully and pressed
A crucifix, in silence, to his breast.
Valdivia, all in burnished steel arrayed,
Upon whose crest the morn's effulgence played,
Majestic reined his steed, and seemed alone,
Worthy the southern world's imperial throne.
His features through the barred casque that glow,
His pole-axe pendent from the saddle-bow;
His dazzling armour, and the glitter bright
Of his drawn sabre, in the orient light,

Speak him not, now, for knightly tournament
Arrayed, but on emprise of prowess bent,
And deeds of deadly strife. In blooming pride,
The attendant youth rode, pensive, by his side.
Their pennoned lances, waving in the wind,
Two hundred clanking horsemen tramped behind,
In iron harness clad. The bugles blew,
And high in air the sanguine ensigns flew.
The arbalasters{j} next, with cross-bows slung,
Marched, whilst the plumed Moors their cymbals swung.
Auxiliar-Indians here, a various train.
With spears and bows, darkened the distant plain;
Drums rolled, and fifes re-echoed shrill and clear,
At intervals, as near and yet more near,
While flags and intermingled halberds shine,
The long battalion drew its passing line.
Last rolled the heavy guns, a sable tier,
By Indians drawn, with matchmen in the rear;
And many a straggling mule and sumpter-train
Closed the embattled order on the plain,
Till nought beneath the azure sky appears
But the projecting points of scarce-discovered spears,
Slow up the hill, with floating vapours hoar,
Or by the blue lake's long retiring shore,
Now seen distinct, through the disparting haze,
The glittering file its bannered length displays;
Now winding from the woods, again appears
The moving line of matchlocks and of spears.
Part seen, part lost; the long illustrious march
Circling the swamp, now draws its various arch;
And seems, as on it moves, meandering slow,
A radiant segment of a living bow.

Five days the Spaniards, trooping in array,
O'er plains and headlands, held their eastern way.
On the sixth early dawn, with shuddering awe
And horror, in the last defile they saw
Ten pendent heads, from which the gore still run,
All gashed, and grim, and blackening in the sun.
These were the gallant troop that passed before,
The Indians' vast encampment to explore,
Led by Del Oro, now with many a wound
Pierced, and a headless trunk upon the ground.
The horses startled, as they tramped in blood;
The troops a moment half-recoiling stood.

But boots not now to pause, or to retire;
Valdivia's eye flashed with indignant fire:

Follow! he cried, brave comrades, to the hill!
And instant shouts the pealing valley fill.

And now, up to the hill's ascending crest,
With animated look and beating breast,
He urged his steed; when, wide beneath his eye,
He saw, in long expanse, Arauco's valley lie.
Far as the labouring sight could stretch its glance,
One undulating mass of club and lance,
One animated surface seemed to fill
The many-stirring scene from hill to hill:
To the deep mass he pointed with his sword,
Banner, advance! give out "Castile!" the word.

Instant the files advance, the trumpets bray,
And now the host in terrible array,
Ranged on the heights that overlook the plain,
Has halted!

But the task were long and vain
To tell what nations, from the seas that roar
Round Patagonia's melancholy shore;
From forests, brown with everlasting shades;
From rocks of sunshine, white with prone cascades;
From snowy summits, where the Llama roams,
Oft bending o'er the cataract as it foams;
From streams whose bridges tremble from the steep;
From lakes, in summer's sweetest light asleep;
Indians, of sullen brow and giant limb,
With clubs terrific, and with aspects grim,
Flocked fearless.

When they saw the Spanish line
Arrayed, and front to front, descending shine,
Burst, instant burst, the universal cry,
(Ten thousand spears uplifted to the sky)—
Tyrants, we come to conquer or to die!

Grim Mariantu led the Indian force
A-left; and, rushing to the foremost horse,
Hurled with unerring aim the involving thong,
Then fearless sprang amidst the mailed throng.

Valdivia saw the horse, entangled, reel,
And shouting, as he rode, Castile! Castile!
Led on the charge: like a descending flood,
It swept, till every spur was black with blood.
His force a-right, where Harratomac led,

A thousand spears went hissing overhead,
And feathered arrows, of each varying hue,
In glancing arch, beneath the sunbeams flew.
Dire was the strife, when ardent Teucapel
Advancing in the front of carnage fell.
At once, Ongolmo, Elicura, rushed,
And swaying their huge clubs together, crushed
Horseman and horse; then bathed their hands in gore,
And limb from limb the panting carcase tore.
Caupolican, where the main battle bleeds,
Hosts and succeeding hosts undaunted leads,
Till, torn and shattered by the ceaseless fire,
Thousands, with gnashing teeth, and clenched spears, expire.
Pierced by a hundred wounds, Ongolmo lies,
And grasps his club terrific as he dies.

With breathless expectation, on the height,
Lautaro watched the long and dubious fight:
Pale and resigned the meek man stood, and pressed
More close the holy image to his breast.
Now nearer to the fight Lautaro drew,
When on the ground a warrior met his view,
Upon whose features memory seemed to trace
A faint resemblance of his father's face;
O'er him a horseman, with collected might,
Raised his uplifted sword, in act to smite,
When the youth springing on, without a word,
Snatched from a soldier's wearied grasp his sword,
And smote the horseman through the crest: a yell
Of triumph burst, as to the ground he fell.
Lautaro{k} shouted, On! brave brothers, on!
Scatter them like the snow!—the day is won!
Lo, I! Lautaro{k},—Attacapac's son!

The Indians turn: again the battle bleeds,
Cleft are the helms and crushed the struggling steeds.
The bugle sounds, and faint with toil and heat,
Some straggling horsemen to the hills retreat.
Stand, brave companions! bold Valdivia cried,
And shook his sword, in recent carnage dyed;
Oh! droop not—droop not yet—all is not o'er—
Brave, faithful friends, one glorious sally more.
Where is Lautaro! leaps his willing sword
Now to avenge his long-indulgent lord!
He waited not for answer, but again
Spurred to the centre of the horrid plain.
Clubs, arrows, spears, the spot of death inclose,
And fainter now the Spanish shouts arose.

'Mid ghastly heaps of many a bleeding corse,
Lies the caparisoned and dying horse.

While still the rushing multitudes assail,
Vain is the fiery tube, the twisted mail!
The Spanish horsemen faint; long yells resound,
As the dragged ensign trails the gory ground:
Shout, for the chief is seized!—a thousand cries
Burst forth—Valdivia! for the sacrifice!
And lo, in silent dignity resigned,
The meek Anselmo, led in bonds, behind!
His hand upon his breast, young Zarinel
Amidst a group of mangled Indians fell;
The spear that to his heart a passage found
Left poor Olola's hair within the wound.

Now all is hushed, save where, at times, alone,
Deep midnight listens to a distant moan;
Save where the condors clamour, overhead,
And strike with sounding beaks the helmets of the dead.

NOTES

It may be necessary here to say, that whenever the Spaniards founded a city, after the immediate walls of defence, their first object was to build a church, and to have, with as much pomp as possible, the ecclesiastical services performed. Hence the cathedrals founded by them in America were of transcendent beauty and magnificence.

Almagro, who first penetrated into Chili, was afterwards strangled.

Pizarro was assassinated.

Rude hanging bridges, constructed by the natives.

CANTO EIGHTH

ARGUMENT

Indian festival for victory—Old Warrior brought in wounded—Recognises his long-lost son, and dies—Discovery—Conclusion with the Old Warrior's funeral, and prophetic oration by the Missionary

The morn returns, and, reddening, seems to shed
One ray of glory on the patriot-dead.
Round the dark stone, the victor-chiefs behold!
Still on their locks the gouts of gore hang cold!

There stands the brave Caupolican, the pride
Of Chili, young Lautaro, by his side!
Near the grim circle, pendent from the wood,
Twelve hundred Spanish heads are dripping blood.
Shrill sound the notes of death: in festive dance,
The Indian maids with myrtle boughs advance;
The tinkling sea-shells on their ancles ring,
As, hailing thus the victor-youth, they sing:—

SONG OF INDIAN MAIDS.

Oh, shout for Lautaro, the young and the brave!
The arm of whose strength was uplifted to save,
When the steeds of the strangers came rushing amain,
And the ghosts of our fathers looked down on the slain!

'Twas eve, and the noise of the battle was o'er,
Five thousand brave warriors were cold in their gore;
When, in front, young Lautaro invincible stood,
And the horses and iron-men rolled in their blood!

As the snows of the mountain are swept by the blast,
The earthquake of death o'er the white men has passed;
Shout, Chili, in triumph! the battle is won,
And we dance round the heads that are black in the sun!

Lautaro, as if wrapt in thought profound,
Oft turned an anxious look inquiring round.
He is not here!—Say, does my father live?
Ere eager voices could an answer give,
With faltering footsteps and declining head,
And slowly by an aged Indian led,
Wounded and weak the mountain chief appears:
Live, live! Lautaro cried, with bursting tears,
And fell upon his neck, and, kissing, pressed,
With folding arms, his gray hairs to his breast.
Oh, live! I am thy son—thy long-lost child!
The warrior raised his look, and faintly smiled;
Chili, my country, is avenged! he cried:
My son!—then sunk upon a shield—and died.

Lautaro knelt beside him, as he bowed,
And kissed his bleeding breast, and wept aloud.
The sounds of sadness through the circle ran,
When thus, with lifted axe, Caupolican:
What, for our fathers, brothers, children, slain,
Canst thou repay, ruthless, inhuman Spain?
Here, on the scene with recent slaughter red,

To sooth the spirits of the brave who bled,
Raise we, to-day, the war-feast of the dead.
Bring forth the chief in bonds! Fathers, to-day
Devote we to our gods the noblest prey!

Lautaro turned his eyes, and, gazing round,
Beheld Valdivia and Anselmo bound!
One stood in arms, as with a stern despair,
His helmet cleft in twain, his temples bare,
Where streaks of blood that dropped upon his mail,
Served but to show his face more deadly pale:
His eyebrows, dark and resolute, he bent,
And stood, composed, to wait the dire event.

Still on the cross his looks Anselmo cast,
As if all thought of this vain world was passed,
And in a world of light, without a shade,
Ev'n now his meek and guileless spirit strayed.
Where stood the Spanish chief, a muttering sound
Rose, and each club was lifted from the ground;
When, starting from his father's corse, his sword
Waving before his once-triumphant lord,
Lautaro cried, My breast shall meet the blow:
But save—save him, to whom my life I owe!

Valdivia marked him with unmoving eye,
Then looked upon his bonds, nor deigned reply;
When Harratomac, stealing with slow pace,
And lifting high his iron-jagged mace,
Smote him to earth; a thousand voices rose,
Mingled with shouts and yells, So fall our foes!

Lautaro gave to tears a moment's space,
As black in death he marked Valdivia's face,
Then cried—Chiefs, friends, and thou, Caupolican,
Oh, spare this innocent and holy man!
He never sailed, rapacious, o'er the deep,
The gold of blood-polluted lands to heap;
He never gave the armed hosts his aid,
But meekly to the Mighty Spirit prayed,
That in all lands the sounds of woe might cease,
And brothers of the wide world dwell in peace!
The victor-youth saw generous sympathy
Already steal to every warrior's eye;
Then thus again: Oh, if this filial tear
Bear witness my own father was most dear;
If this uplifted arm, this bleeding steel
Speak for my country what I felt and feel;

If, at this hour, I meet her high applause,
While my heart beats still ardent in her cause;—
Hear, and forgive these tears that grateful flow,
Oh! hear, how much to this poor man I owe!

I was a child—when to my sire's abode,
In Chillan's vale, the armed horsemen rode:
Me, whilst my father cold and breathless lay,
Far off the crested soldiers bore away,
And for a captive sold. No friend was near,
To mark a young and orphan stranger's tear!
This humble man, with kind parental care,
Snatched me from slavery—saved from dark despair;
And as my years increased, protected, fed,
And breathed a father's blessings on my head.
A Spanish maid was with him: need I speak?
Behold, affection's tear still wets my cheek!
Years, as they passed, matured in ripening grace
Her form unfolding, and her beauteous face:
She heard my orphan tale; she loved to hear,
And sometimes for my fortunes dropped a tear.
I could have bowed to direst ills resigned,
But wept at looks so sweet, at words so kind.

Valdivia saw me, now in blooming age,
And claimed me from the father as his page;
The chief too cherished me, yea, saved my life,
When in Peru arose the civil strife.
Yet still remembering her I loved so well,
Oft I returned to the gray father's cell:
His voice instructed me; recalled my youth
From rude idolatry to heavenly truth:
Of this hereafter; he my darkling mind
Cleared, and from low and sensual thoughts refined.
Then first, with feelings new impressed, I strove
To hide the tear of tenderness and love:
Amid the fairest maidens of Peru,
My eyes, my heart, one only object knew:
I lived that object's love and faith to share;
He saw, and blessed us with a father's prayer.

Here, at Valdivia's last and stern command,
I came, a stranger in my native land!
Anselmo (so him call—now most in need—
And standing here in bonds, for whom I plead)
Came, by our chief so summoned, and for aid
To the Great Spirit of the Christians prayed:
Here as a son I loved him, but I left

A wife, a child, of my fond cares bereft,
Never to see again; for death awaits
My entrance now in Lima's jealous gates.

Caupolican, didst thou thy father love?
Did his last dying look affection move?
Pity this aged man; unbend thy brow:
He was my father—is my father, now!
Consenting mercy marks each warrior's mien.
But who is this, what pallid form is seen,
As crushed already by the fatal blow,
Bound, and with looks white as a wreath of snow,
Her hands upon her breast, scarce drawn her breath,
A Spanish woman knelt, expecting death,
Whilst, borne by a dark warrior at her side,
An infant shrunk from the red plumes, and cried!
Lautaro started:

Injured maid of Spain!
Me!—me! oh, take me to thine arms again!
She heard his voice, and, by the scene oppressed,
With one faint sigh fell senseless on his breast.

Caupolican, with warm emotion, cried,
Live, live! Lautaro and his beauteous bride!
Live, aged father!—and forthwith commands
A warrior to unbind Anselmo's hands.
She raised her head: his eyes first met her view,
As round Lautaro's neck her arms she threw,
Ah, no! she feebly spoke; it is not true!
It is some form of the distempered brain!
Then hid her face upon his breast again.

Dark flashing eyes, terrific, glared around:
Here, his brains scattered by the deadly wound,
The Spanish chief lay on the gory ground.
With lowering brows, and mace yet drooping blood,
And clotted hair, there Mariantu stood.
Anselmo here, sad, yet in sorrow mild,
Appeared: she cried, A blessing on your child,
And knelt, as slow revived her waking sense,
And then, with looks aghast, Oh bear us hence!
Now all the assembled chiefs, assenting, cried,
Live, live! Lautaro and his beauteous bride!
With eager arms Lautaro snatched his boy,
And kissed him in an agony of joy;
Then to Anselmo gave, who strove to speak,
And felt the tear first burning on his cheek:

The infant held his neck with strict embrace,
And kissed his pale emaciated face.

From the dread scene, wet with Valdivia's gore,
His wan and trembling charge Lautaro bore.
There was a bank, where slept the summer-light,
A small stream whispering went in mazes bright,
And stealing from the sea, the western wind
Waved the magnolias on the slope inclined:
The woodpecker, in glittering plumage green,
And echoing bill, beneath the boughs was seen;
And, arched with gay and pendent flowers above,
The floripondio its rich trellis wove.
Lautaro bent, with looks of love and joy,
O'er his yet trembling wife and beauteous boy:

Oh, by what miracle, beloved! say,
Hast thou escaped the perils of the way
From Lima, where our humble dwelling stood,
To these tumultuous scenes, this vale of blood?

Roused by his voice, as from the sleep of death,
Faint she replied, with slow-recovering breath,
Who shall express, when thou, best friend! wert gone,
How sunk my heart!—deserted and alone!
Would I were with thee! oft I sat and sighed,
When the pale moon shone on the silent tide—
At length resolved, I sought thee o'er the seas:
The brave bark cheer'ly went before the breeze,
That arms and soldiers to Valdivia bore,
From Lima bound to Chili's southern shore:
I seized the fair occasion—ocean smiled,
As to the sire I bore his lisping child.
The storm arose: with loud and sudden shock
The vessel sunk, disparting on a rock.
Some mariners, amidst the billows wild,
Scarce saved, in one small boat, me and my child.
What I have borne, a captive since that day—
Forgive these tears—I scarce have heart to say!
None pitied, save one gentle Indian maid—
A wild maid—of her looks I was afraid;
Her long black hair upon her shoulders fell,
And in her hand she bore a wreathed shell.

Lautaro for a moment turned aside,
And, Oh, my sister! with faint voice he cried.

Already free from sorrow and alarms,

I clasped in thought a husband in my arms,
When a dark warrior, stationed on the height,
Who held his solitary watch by night,
Before me stood, and lifting high his lance,
Exclaimed: No further, on thy life, advance!
Faint, wearied, sinking to the earth with dread,
Back to the dismal cave my steps he led.
Only at eve, within the craggy cleft,
Some water, and a cake of maize, were left.
The thirteenth sun unseen went down the sky;
When morning came, they brought me forth to die;
But hushed be every sigh, each boding fear,
Since all I sought on earth, and all I love, is here!

Her infant raised his hands, with glistening eye,
To reach a large and radiant butterfly,
That fluttered near his face; with looks of love,
And truth and tenderness, Lautaro strove
To calm her wounded heart; the holy sire,
His eyes faint-lighted with a transient fire,
Hung o'er them, and to Heaven his prayer addressed,
While, with uplifted hands, he wept and blest.
An aged Indian came, with feathers crowned,
And knelt before Lautaro on the ground.
What tidings, Indian?

INDIAN
When I led thy sire,
Whom late thou saw'st upon his shield expire,
Son of our Ulmen, didst thou mark no trace,
In these sad looks, of a remembered face?
Dost thou remember Izdabel? Look here!
It is thy father's hatchet and his spear.
Friend of my infant days, how I rejoice,
Lautaro cried, once more to hear that voice!
Life like a dream, since last we met, has fled—
Oh, my beloved sister, thou art dead!

INDIAN
I come to guide thee through untrodden ways,
To the lone valley, where thy father's days
Were passed; where every cave and every tree,
From morn to morn, reminded him of thee!

Lautaro cried: Here, faithful Indian, stay;
I have a last sad duty yet to pay.
A little while we part:—thou here remain.
He spake, and passed like lightning o'er the plain.

Ah, cease, Castilian maid, thy vain alarms!
See where he comes—his father in his arms!

Now lead, he cried. The Indian, sad and still,
Paced on from wood to vale, from vale to hill;
Her infant tired, and hushed a while to rest,
Smiled, in a dream, upon its mother's breast;
The pensive mother gray Anselmo led;
Behind, Lautaro bore his father dead.

Beneath the branching palms they slept at night;
The small birds waked them ere the morning light.
Before their path, in distant view, appeared
The mountain-smoke, that its dark column reared
O'er Andes' summits, in the pale blue sky,
Lifting their icy pinnacles so high.
Four days they onward held their eastern way;
On the fifth rising morn, before them lay
Chillan's lone glen, amid whose windings green,
The Warrior's loved and last abode was seen.
No smoke went up, a stillness reigned around,
Save where the waters fell with soothing sound,
Save where the Thenca sang so loud and clear,
And the bright humming-bird was spinning near.
Yet here all human tumults seemed to cease,
And sunshine rested on the spot of peace;
The myrtles bloomed as fragrant and as green
As if Lautaro scarce had left the scene;
And in his ear the falling waters' spray
Seemed swelling with the sounds of yesterday.

Where yonder rock the aged cedars shade,
There shall my father's bones in peace be laid.

Beneath the cedar's shade they dug the ground;
The small and sad communion gathered round.
Beside the grave stood aged Izdabel,
And broke the spear, and cried: Farewell, farewell!
Lautaro hid his face, and sighed Adieu!
As the stone hatchet in the grave he threw.
The little child that to its mother clung,
Stretched out its arm, then on her garment hung,
With sidelong looks, half-shrinking, half-amazed,
And dropped its flowers, unconscious, as it gazed.

And now Anselmo, his pale brow inclined,
The honoured relics, dust to dust, consigned
With Christian rites, and sung, on bending knee,

"Eternam pacem dona, Domine."
Then rising up he closed the holy book;
And lifting in the beam his lighted look,
(The cross, with meekness, folded on his breast),
Here, too, he cried, my bones in peace shall rest!
Few years remain to me, and never more
Shall I behold, O Spain! thy distant shore!
Here lay my bones, that the same tree may wave
O'er the poor Christian's and the Indian's grave.
Oh, may it (when the sons of future days
Shall hear our tale and on the hillock gaze),
Oh, may it teach, that charity should bind,
Where'er they roam, the brothers of mankind!
The time shall come, when wildest tribes shall hear
Thy voice, O Christ! and drop the slaughtering spear.

Yet we condemn not him who bravely stood,
To seal his country's freedom with his blood;
And if, in after-times, a ruthless band
Of fell invaders sweep my native land,
May she, by Chili's stern example led,
Hurl back his thunder on the assailant's head;
Sustained by Freedom, strike the avenging blow,
And learn one virtue from her ancient foe!

William Lisle Bowles – A Short Biography

William Lisle Bowles was born on 24th September 1762 at King's Sutton in Northamptonshire.

His great-grandfather, grandfather and his father, William Thomas Bowles, had all been parish priests and inevitably Bowles would join their line.

At the age of 14 he entered Winchester College, where the headmaster was Dr Joseph Warton (a minor poet, his most notable piece is The Enthusiast, 1744. In 1755, he taught at Winchester and from 1766 to 1793 was headmaster. His career as a critic was illustrious. He produced editions of poets such as Virgil as well as several English poets).

In 1789 Bowles published, a small quarto volume, Fourteen Sonnets, which was received with extraordinary praise, not only by the general public, but by such revered poets as Samuel Taylor Coleridge and Wordsworth.

The Sonnets were a return to an older and purer poetic style, and by their grace of expression, lyrical versification, tender tone of feeling and vivid appreciation of the wonder and beauty of nature, stood out in marked contrast to the elaborate works which then formed the bulk of English poetry.

Bowles said "Poetic trifles from solitary rambles whilst chewing the cud of sweet and bitter fancy, written from memory, confined to fourteen lines, this seemed best adapted to the unity of sentiment, the verse flowed in unpremeditated harmony as my ear directed but are far from being mere elegiac couplets".

The young Samuel Taylor Coleridge felt obliged to record his debt of gratitude to Bowles: "My obligations to Mr. Bowles were indeed important, and for radical good. At a very premature age, ... I had bewildered myself in metaphysicks, and in theological controversy. Nothing else pleased me. Poetry ... became insipid to me.... This preposterous pursuit was, beyond doubt, injurious both to my natural powers, and to the progress of my education.... But from this I was auspiciously withdrawn, chiefly by the genial influence of a style of poetry, so tender and yet so manly, so natural and real, and yet so dignified and harmonious, as the sonnets &c. of Mr. Bowles!"

In 1781 Bowles left as captain of Winchester school, and proceeded to Trinity College, Oxford, after winning a scholarship. Two years later he won the Chancellor's prize for Latin verse. It was now evident that the Church and poetry were to be his two callings.

After receiving his degree at Oxford, Bowles now began his career in service to the Church of England. In 1792, after serving as curate in Donhead St Andrew, Bowles was appointed vicar of Chicklade in Wiltshire.

Five years later, in 1797, he received the vicarage of Dumbleton in Gloucestershire, and in 1804 became vicar of Bremhill in Wiltshire, where he wrote the poem seen on Maud Heath's statue. In the same year his bishop, John Douglas, collated him to a prebendal stall in Salisbury Cathedral.

In 1818 Bowles was made chaplain to the Prince Regent, and in 1828 he was elected residentiary canon of Salisbury.

His years of service perhaps diminished both his stature as a poet and certainly the way he was viewed. For much of his career Bowles was seen as rather soft when set against his contemporaries but in the end his ability as a poet was enshrined, after a long and ferocious attack against him, by the principles he so eloquently wrote about and adhered too.

It is as well to remember that when critics suggest that compared to other poets his longer works were not to the standard that the competition achieved, that this era is perhaps without poetic equal. Set against Byron, Shelley, Keats, Wordsworth and other great luminaries of the era it is perhaps difficult to see his works in isolation for their own value.

The longer poems published by Bowles are distinguished by purity of imagination, cultured and graceful diction, and a great thoughtfulness of feeling. Among them were The Spirit of Discovery (1804), which alas was so mercilessly ridiculed by Byron; The Missionary (1813); The Grave of the Last Saxon (1822); and St John in Patmos (1833).

In 1806 he published an edition of Alexander Pope's works with notes and an essay, in which he laid down certain canons as to poetic imagery which, subject to some modification, were later accepted, but received at the time with strong opposition by admirers of Pope.

Bowles restated his views in 1819, in The Invariable Principles of Poetry. The controversy brought into sharp contrast the opposing views of poetry, which may be thought of as being either the natural or the artificial.

In personality and nature Bowles was said to be an amiable, absent-minded, but rather eccentric man. His poems speak warmly of a refinement of feeling, tenderness, and pensive thought, but are lacking in power and passion. But that should not diminish their value or appreciation to us.

Bowles maintained that images drawn from nature are poetically finer than those drawn from art; and that in the highest kinds of poetry the themes or passions handled should be of the general or elemental kind, and not the transient manners of any society. These positions were attacked by Byron, Thomas Campbell, William Roscoe and others, and for a time Bowles had to fight his corner on his own. Soon however, William Hazlitt and the Blackwood critics came to his assistance, and on the whole Bowles had reason to congratulate himself on having established certain principles which might serve as the basis of a true method of poetical criticism, and of having inaugurated, both by precept and by example, a new era in English poetry.

As well as his poetry Bowles was also responsible for writing a Life of Bishop Ken (in two volumes, 1830–1831), Coombe Ellen and St. Michael's Mount (1798), The Battle of the Nile (1799), and The Sorrows of Switzerland (1801).

Bowles also enjoyed considerable reputation as an antiquary and his principal work in that field was Hermes Britannicus (1828).

William Lisle Bowles died on April 7th, 1850 at the age of 87.

www.ingramcontent.com/pod-product-compliance
Lightning Source LLC
Chambersburg PA
CBHW060053050426
42448CB00011B/2431